()

A Cut Above

A Cut Above

SIDNEY OWITZ

authorHOUSE®

AuthorHouse™
1663 Liberty Drive
Bloomington, IN 47403
www.authorhouse.com
Phone: 1 (800) 839-8640

Published by AuthorHouse 11/06/2015

ISBN: 978-1-5049-6077-9 (sc)
ISBN: 978-1-5049-6078-6 (hc)
ISBN: 978-1-5049-6076-2 (e)

Print information available on the last page.

Table of Contents

Dedication

This book is dedicated to my wife, Joan, and children, Stephanie, Valerie, David, Darron, Carole, Robin and Jeff

CHAPTER 1

Holier Than Thou

History is full of patriots who have led their countries in war and in peace, people who have loved the land of their birth and given their lives for their motherland or fatherland, people whose first calling was to preserve the soil of their ancestors. They display with pride the family trees of their forebears who had grown and flourished on the same soil almost forever. Who could blame them for their heroism and patriotism? Yet there have also been those who were not born in the land for which they have fought and protected and given their lives. They are aliens from foreign soil who have devoted themselves to their adopted countries, lands to which they had no ancestral heritage - perhaps they had even been war-time enemies of old. What causes an alien to devote his life to another man's land? From whence cometh the spark that would cause their lives to outshine those of the natives of the land of their adoption?

Catherine the Great, Empress of Russia, was a Prussian who had no attachments to Russia. Russia and Prussia had been enemies on many occasions in the past. Yet she became the ruler of Russia, and during her reign Russia made huge strides in development as a major European power. She was the longest reigning ruler in the history of Russia and was responsible for expanding the size of this already huge country. Napoleon Bonaparte was probably the greatest hero in the history of France. He is still spoken of in awe by the French, but he was not a son of France. He was the conqueror of Europe and he introduced the Code

Napoleon, which many countries still follow. Adolf Hitler, an Austrian by birth, became the Fuehrer of Germany. He conquered most of Europe in World War II and almost succeeded in destroying European Jewry. As Roosevelt said, his name will live in infamy. Saladin, a Kurd from Mesopotamia, became the Sultan of Egypt and, later, leader of the Muslim Empire in the 12th century, ruling over the Middle East from Egypt to as far as Mesopotamia. During the 20th century Dr. Hendrik Verwoerd, a Dutchman born in the Netherlands and who spent many years in Rhodesia (Zimbabwe today) became Prime Minister of South Africa. He was the author of the policy of Apartheid, helped to change the constitution in order to transform South Africa into a Republic, and became its first President. Golda Meir was born in Kiev, in the Ukraine, and she became the first female Prime Minister of Israel. Eamon de Valera, born in the USA, became the first president of Eire. These are all strange people who became patriots of foreign lands. Of course, this could not happen in the United States where the President must be born on United States soil.

Catherine the Great

Catherine the Great lived from 1720 to 1796. She was born to a ruling family in Prussia. The Royal families of Europe were constantly arranging marriages with each other for the purpose of military or political alliances and for reasons of security or in order to extend their territorial ambitions. Thus it was arranged by the reigning Empress Elizabeth of Russia for Sophia of Prussia (who changed her name to Catherine) to marry her nephew Peter who would one day become Tsar Peter III. After arriving in St. Petersburg Catherine said that she detested Peter, but they nevertheless married. This was a job that had to be done. Peter was not a normal person. He had some developmental problems and never really grew up. Even when he became an adult he would play with toy soldiers, and often arranged for the staff of the palace to play in war games with him. His relationship with Catherine was never smooth, and they often lived apart from each other. When the Empress Dowager Elizabeth (his aunt) died Peter succeeded her to the throne. His reign lasted only six months. He idolized the Prussian army; this was contrary to the views of the Russian leaders who in the past had looked upon the Prussians as dangerous enemies. Peter was not popular, and a coup was plotted against him, and later he was assassinated. It is said by many sources of information that Catherine had a hand in his ouster and assassination. She followed him on the throne as Catherine II, just as Catherine I had followed Peter the Great. She did not marry again after Peter's death, preferring to remain Empress of Russia without any spousal escort, although her sexual encounters have given rise to much gossip.

There were some rough periods that she went through at the commencement of her reign, as there were a few attempted coups against her, but they were overcome by the military, whose officers she had already befriended. The Cossacks attempted a march on the capital intending to overthrow Catherine, but her loyal army easily neutralized them.

Catherine received no love from Peter while he was alive, but apparently had lovers amongst the officers in the army whom she was always supplying with gifts and money, high governmental positions, even thrones, such as the throne of the Kingdom of Poland which she gave to her lover, Stanislav. She became notorious for her lovers chosen from the military and also from amongst her advisers. Other lovers included Grigory Potemkin who moved into her palace and participated in many decisions of national importance.

She joined the Orthodox Church against the wishes of her family in Prussia, who were Lutherans. Religion, however, did not appear to be important to her. She reduced the powers of the clergy. She learnt to speak Russian, but always spoke it with a heavy foreign accent. She taxed Jews in her kingdom twice as much as ethnic Russians, and she was tolerant towards Muslims in her land. She believed that serfdom was inhuman, but she did nothing to end the custom as this would have created a furor amongst the wealthy, and she needed their support.

During her reign Russia increased in size as a result of wars against the Ottoman Empire. She gained the Crimean Peninsula, some of the Caucasus and the land around the Sea of Azov. Belarus and Lithuania were also added to her realm. From then on the Ottoman Empire gradually weakened and became known as 'the sick man of Europe'. She fought wars against Sweden and Denmark; she gained the greater part of Poland and divided up the land with Prussia and Austria, taking the lion's share for herself; she gained entry into Japan before any other country was able to do so, and almost completed a trade agreement with the Japanese who historically had shunned all foreigners. She started a Russian colonization of Alaska, giving her entrance into the North American continent.

She was a follower of the Enlightenment. She added many works of art to the Hermitage Museum in St. Petersburg, and it was her introductions of art masterpieces to the Hermitage that forms the basis of its collection. She bought up valuable collections from famous art collectors in other European lands, including England and France, and saw to it that the Hermitage would be the finest museum in the world. She also did a great deal for education for the Russian people and encouraged them to turn their attention in those directions. She was in contact continuously by mail with the French thinkers, Voltaire and Diderot. When she heard that Diderot was in severe financial straits she bought up his library so he could pay his debts, and when Diderot wanted to deliver all its contents to Russia she said that the library should remain intact where it was and she would call for it when she required it – she never did! She invited Diderot to come to Russia in order to do some of his writing there, which he did. They spent a great deal of time together indulging in philosophical discussions.

Her reign was considered to be the Golden Age of Russia. She modernized and Westernized Russia. She bridged the gulf between Europe and the large bounding territory of the Russian steppes and snow-bound land that extended across two continents. At the time of her death Russia had become one of the greatest and most respected powers of Europe. She was a foreigner with no Russian heredity or influence during her upbringing or any time in her life, and yet she became more Russian than the Russians. Her legacy was unequalled by any other czar or leader either before or since. She was also the longest reigning monarch in Russian history. When she died in 1796 she was followed by her son Paul who was probably not fathered by Peter.

Napoleon

Napoleon Bonaparte was born in 1769 in Ajaccio on the island of Corsica. Historically it had always been a part of Italy, a member of the nation-state of Genoa. Italy had not been unified as one country yet. He spoke Corsican which was like Tuscan, similar to modern Italian; his parents were Italian. France took over Corsica a year before he was born. His father, Carlo, did not resist the invasion, and Napoleon later resented his father for this. However, they moved to France when Napoleon was about nine where he was teased for his foreign accent which apparently remained with him forever. He did not like the French and did not like France, and when the French Revolution broke out in 1789 he returned to Corsica. Here he met Pasquale Paoli, his hero and Corsica's anti-French firebrand. Napoleon worshipped Pasquale and was prepared to follow him. He fought beside him, guerilla-style, against the French occupation, but after a while he felt that the past should be forgotten and French leadership should be accepted. With their disagreement, he and Paoli had a 'falling out' and parted. Thereupon, Napoleon returned to France.

France was in the midst of a reign of terror under Robespierre. The king and queen had gone to the guillotine, the 1st estate (clergy) and the 2nd estate (nobility) lost their privileges. A counter-revolution was starting in the south of France while the British took possession of the port at Toulon. Robespierre and the Jacobins began to notice the young new lieutenant, and he was sent with a number of troops to re-take Toulon port. Instead of trying to take over the port held by the British, a maneuver which would probably have failed, he took over the surrounding hill-tops, and from there bombarded the town. He then started bombing the British ships. The British retreated, and Napoleon was promoted to general. With no previous experience in organized battle he displayed an amazing genius for warfare.

In 1794 the reign of terror by Robespierre and the Jacobins ended. Napoleon was arrested and jailed for being an associate of Robespierre. The new regime, known as the Directory, did not want to have anything to do with him. However, when a royalist insurrection was threatened and it appeared that there may be difficulty in maintaining control they called upon Napoleon to crush the coup. He did so instantly, and this success brought him further promotion from Barras and Marat, the Directory leaders. He was made leader of the French army in Italy.

There had been an ongoing war between France and Austria since 1792. The northern part of Italy belonged to Austria. With a small army, under-fed and without pay he waged a lightning campaign and defeated the Austrians on Italian soil. By his actions he forced Austria to cede its Italian territory to France, thereby creating the Cisalpine Republic.

Returning as a conquering hero he was given the command to attack England, always a thorn in the side of France. Nothing came of this as the task appeared to be insurmountable, but instead Napoleon decided to attack Egypt as this would disrupt the sea-lanes for British ships going to India and the Orient thereby interfering with their economy and embarrassing their Navy. This was an alternative method, he thought, for defeating the arch-enemy. Egypt was a province of the Ottoman Empire. He took his troops to Egypt and won the Battle of the Pyramids. He then entered Cairo, but the British navy under Nelson defeated him at the Battle of the Nile. This was a severe impediment to his plans, yet all was not lost because he had brought scholars with him to Egypt, and the study of Egyptology had its foundations with Napoleon's entry into Egypt. It led to the discovery of the Rosetta Stone, hieroglyphics and the ancient tombs of the pharaohs. The study of hieroglyphics opened up the pages of antiquity and introduced great details of the ancient history of Egypt, which had been lost through the ages. In years to come numerous scholars from France and England followed in Napoleon's footsteps and furthered the study of Ancient Egypt.

While in Egypt he set up headquarters in Cairo where he ruled the land. In the meantime the Sultan of the Ottoman Empire, hearing of some of the defeats of Napoleon incurred on him by the British fleet, sent troops to Syria and Palestine to attack the French army in Egypt. Napoleon, when he heard of this, decided to pre-empt the Ottoman forces and sent his men to Jaffa, Gaza and Acre to foil any Ottoman incursion.

He had intended to invade India as well, but disgraced by his loss at the Battle of the Nile he slipped out of Egypt without his army by eluding the British. His soldiers were expected to find their own way home; this was not considered to be a leadership quality. He had to return to Paris because he was seeking more power and he had reason to believe that his wife, Josephine, was cheating on him.

On his return he found that the Directory had been overthrown by a coup and replaced by a Consulate of three people. He complained that he had left a peaceful France when he went to Egypt, and in his absence all hell had broken loose. He made himself one of the Consuls – for life, with near-dictatorial powers. He found himself as the most important person in France! He was hailed as a benevolent leader. The Code Napoleon was his greatest achievement. It dealt with civil rights, marriage and divorce and inheritance. It was taken to all the European countries that he conquered, and would be introduced to all future lands that would become a part of his Empire. He abolished all remnants of feudalism. He created legal equality for all people and supported religious tolerance.

Yet he had problems with the Catholic Church. In 1796 on his excursion through Italy he over-ran the Papal States and declared the Republic of Rome. Pope Pius VI would not renounce his authority, whereby Napoleon had him jailed; he died six months later. Pope Pius VII followed him. Napoleon demanded Vatican support and the Pope wished for freedom of the Papal States. They made a peace plan (or Concordat) –the Pope would be allowed freedom to rule but Napoleon would appoint the bishops. However in 1808 the Papal States were invaded again, the Pope was imprisoned for six years, and only freed by the British after Napoleon was defeated and sent to Elba.

Napoleon was popular with the Jews. He freed them from their ghettos and granted them equality with all other people. He made the

Jewish religion equal in status with Catholicism and Protestantism. It is true that he disliked usury and wanted it ended. It is said that he wanted the Jews to assimilate so that they would be dissolved amongst the masses and not remain a separate nation.

He sold Louisiana to Jefferson because the Haitians gained their independence from France, and it would be too difficult and costly to rule only one territory in the Western Hemisphere from so far away. In 1804 he proclaimed the 1st French Empire, naming himself King of France and King of Italy. When Pius VII came to place the crown on his head at the coronation it is said that Napoleon grabbed the crown from his hands and crowned himself! At first he was most popular with the people and looked upon as a hero, but he later became a dictator. Beethoven composed the Eroica (third symphony) for him, but at a later date when his despotic powers became visible he deleted Napoleon's name from the dedication.

He defeated the Prussians and the Russians at Austerlitz in 1804 (the battle of the three emperors), but Nelson defeated him at sea at the Battle of Trafalgar in 1805. This defeat was so decisive that Napoleon was convinced that there was no way that he could invade Britain. There must be another way to defeat the English apart from invasion, especially after his losses at the Battle of the Nile and Trafalgar.

In 1806 he encountered the Prussians at the Battle of Jena and won again. With most of Europe under his control he used family members and men closest to him to fill the thrones and high positions of state in European lands so that he had a hand in the governing of almost all European countries.

In 1806 he introduced an embargo on Britain so as to fight them economically since he could not defeat them in war. Portugal and Russia would not join him in the embargo, hence the Peninsular War and the March on Moscow. Both these wars were unsuccessful and so commenced the decline of Napoleon. The Peninsular War turned out to be a long drawn-out campaign while the British helped the Portuguese to drive the French back. The Russian invasion started with an all-out onslaught and a minimum of Russian resistance. It ended with the retreat of the French after the burning of Moscow when the cold harsh winter drove them back. Only 2% of his men made it back from Russia; thousands died of disease and from the icy conditions, and a large number of men deserted.

Josephine did not produce a son for him, so he divorced her and married Marie Louise, a Hapsburg, who did produce a son for him. He gave Josephine a home to live in and treated her well, making sure that she was comfortable and in need of nothing.

After the retreat from Moscow, Napoleon wanted to re-establish his power by getting control of Germany. The European countries, however, got together at the Battle of Leipzig to defeat Napoleon, who was outnumbered. He suffered his worst defeat at Leipzig. Thereafter France found itself being attacked from all sides, and the European powers advanced relentlessly. Paris fell in 1814, and Napoleon abdicated. He was exiled to Elba. Marie Louise was taken to Austria, and she and her son never saw Napoleon again. His son became a Hapsburg, not a Bonaparte.

Napoleon escaped from Elba. In the meantime, Louis XVIII, another Bourbon, had taken control of France. He sent Marshal Ney to arrest Napoleon, but Ney who had been appointed as a general by Napoleon and was also his friend, would not do it. Ney was later executed. Napoleon ruled for 100 days after his return from Elba, but his rule ended at the Battle of Waterloo where he was defeated by the Duke of Wellington and Marshal Blucher, the Prussian. This time the British accompanied the prisoner, Napoleon, by sea to the remote island of St. Helena in the South Atlantic, so he would never escape again from captivity. There he wrote his memoirs, and died in 1821. This is a swash-buckling story of an Italian from Corsica who hated the French, and yet became their greatest hero of all time!

Hitler

In 1889 Adolf Hitler was born in Braunau Am Inn in Austria, where he spent his early years. He was another example of a foreigner taking over the reins of government of a different country. His family re-located to Bavaria while he was still a child. He had a poor relationship with his father; he wanted to study art and painting against his father's advice. He later went to live in Vienna, where he was able to carry out his wishes. While there he developed a profound hatred for Jews, which apparently was the climate at that time in Vienna.

Before World War I he went back to live in Germany as he did not wish to serve in the Austro-Hungarian army; he considered Austro-Hungary to be a hodgepodge of multiple nationalities. He joined the German army and fought at some famous World War I battle sites, receiving a number of war medals. He came back from the Front without a set purpose in life, but was interested in national-socialism. He formed a political party, which grew mostly as a result of his mesmerizing speeches and magnetic personality. He spoke against the Treaty of Versailles, which all but paralyzed Germany by its heavy war penalties and the insurmountable difficulties inflicted by the Allies on the populace. Germany had been trying to extricate itself with great difficulty from the shackles that the Treaty had placed upon it. Anybody who spoke up against the Treaty at that time was sure of receiving rapt attention. His anti-Semitism grew stronger when he realized that the Bolsheviks, whom he saw as a group consisting mainly of Jews, were trying to unseat the German government and bring Communism to Germany.

He was responsible for the Beer Hall Putsch in Munich where he attempted to take over the Bavarian government by means of a coup. He spoke at the meeting which was held by members of the Bavarian government, and in so doing mesmerized many of them, including Ludendorf, a war hero. He and his followers marched on Munich, but the Weimar government in Berlin received the word of what was happening and immediately sent in troops that set upon the Nazis, which were the members of Hitler's new National Socialist Party. A number were killed, and Hitler was arrested. At the trial he used the opportunity to spread his Nazi propaganda. He was sentenced to jail, and while there he wrote most of his book "Mein Kampf", outlining his plans for a better Germany. His popularity rose while he was in jail as the newspapers quoted his speeches and discussed his patriotism.

Even though the coup attempt failed Hitler's name was brought to the attention of the nation. His book that was written in jail was a recipe for the German people as to how Hitler was going to lead them to their proud future. The failure of the Putsch also led him to believe in taking over the government by lawful means rather than a putsch. His idea for the Putsch had come from Benito Mussolini who prior to that had marched on Rome with success.

In 1925 Hitler renounced his Austrian citizenship. He became stateless until he received German citizenship in 1932. He immediately opposed Paul von Hindenburg in the presidential elections, but lost even though his Nazi Party was the largest. On account of the growing strength of his party he and his friends were able to urge Hindenburg to appoint him as chancellor. However, this resulted in a political stalemate which forced Hitler to ask Hindenburg to dissolve the government and call for new elections. At a meeting before the elections there was a fire in the Reichstag. This prompted Hitler and his cohorts to blame it on the Communists who were a serious opposition to the Nazi Party. Hitler coerced Hindenburg to restrict free speech and curtail the freedom of the press. Most experts believe that the fire was started by Hitler's own Nazi Party. The Communists became extremely unpopular as people began to believe that they had caused the fire. At the polls Hitler won the election for chancellor and proceeded to arrest numerous members of the Communist Party. Hitler was praised for having prevented a Communist take-over of Germany.

Since he did not have an absolute majority he introduced the Enabling Act, whereby he was given increased powers which he used so that he could demolish opposition at will. The rest is history. He outlawed communism, he legislated numerous anti-Semitic laws preventing Jews from remaining in the professions or from living an ordinary life; he attacked the gypsies; he disregarded the Treaty of Versailles and built up the German army and air force whose re-establishment had been prevented by the Treaty. In many ways he re-instituted self-confidence amongst the German people. He was empowering the German people who had felt down-trodden and without energy since the end of World War I. He invigorated a nation. He was looked upon as a hero who would not bow down to the nations of the world and had humiliated Germany. The Germans, at last, were going to take their rightful place as world leaders. When Hindenburg died Hitler took over his powers of head of state.

He marched into Sudetenland, a part of Czechoslovakia which had a large German population, and not long after that he added the whole of Czechoslovakia into Germany's territory. Without losing any time he soon marched into Austria amid cheering and welcoming crowds. Then on September the 1st 1939 he invaded Poland, surprisingly together with his enemy, the USSR. They took over the entire country and divided Poland between them. Of course, this was the beginning of World War II as Britain and France declared war against Germany because they had a pact to defend Poland if it were attacked (even though they did not send troops to defend Poland). The next year saw Hitler's men toppling country after country in Europe, including the Netherlands, Denmark, Norway, Belgium and France until most of Europe became a part of his domain. Only Britain would not surrender despite a constant daily bombardment of British urban populations from the air.

Hitler was having the same trouble with England as Napoleon had had more than a century before. Hitler finally turned his attention away from England and attacked Russia, his enemy (or his friend, if you consider that they carved up Poland together a mere two years prior to the invasion of the Soviet Union). The Germans got as far as Leningrad (St. Petersburg), Moscow and Stalingrad (Volgograd) where their advance was held up, just as Napoleon had been held up. Then the retreat commenced, and did not cease until the Soviets advanced onto German soil and occupied Berlin. History repeats itself!

The writing was on the wall. While the Russians were defending their homeland the Americans, British and their allies defeated the Axis powers in North Africa, and then invaded Sicily and marched up the boot of Italy. On D-Day (July 4, 1944) the Allies stormed the Normandy coast and advanced across France, liberating Paris at the same time. The Russians were invading Germany from the east. From every direction the Nazi war machine became hemmed in. In a last desperate attempt the Germans attacked the Western Allies at the Battle of the Bulge in Belgium, but were soon defeated, and the Allied war machine marched on. Berlin was entered from all directions. Like a Greek tragedy, Hitler committed suicide by taking poison in his bunker, and Germany sued for peace.

Hitler almost succeeded in annihilating the Jews of Europe. Early in his career he decided that the Jews must be destroyed. He did not budge from his original premise. By the time World War II came to an end six million Jews had lost their lives.

We can see the similarities between Hitler and Napoleon. They both conquered most of Europe. Neither of them was able to subjugate Britain who defeated both of them in the end. Neither Napoleon nor Hitler was able to overcome Russia (or the USSR). They could not handle the cold winters or the Russian defenses. Both retreated from Moscow. Napoleon and Hitler seemed to be successful in their African adventures at first, but were driven out by the British (and later by the Americans, in Hitler's case). Both of these larger-than-life figures robbed the art works and historical artifacts of the countries that they invaded. Both were despots. They were both aliens to the land of their adoption, and spoke with foreign accents.

Yet there were also differences between the two. Napoleon was considered a savior, and was one until he became too dictatorial. He ended the French revolution, and is still regarded as a hero in France. Napoleon started off as a positive force, and was loved and respected by most of the masses. Hitler's rule cannot be seen as anything but a force for evil. Few in Germany today consider him to have been a hero; rather he is seen to have almost ruined Germany and Europe. The Code Napoleon was a fine document meant to improve the lives of the people, and was spread throughout Europe. Hitler almost succeeded in annihilating the Jewish people whereas Napoleon did not exploit anti-Semitism or other forms of bigotry. Napoleon was a military genius, while Hitler relied on his generals. However, when these dictators were out of the way sanity descended upon Europe for a while.

Dr. Verwoerd

South Africa is a relatively small country far from the bustling areas of civilizations in Eurasia and the American continent. Events in South Africa do not usually affect the rest of the world. Yet in the field of human rights a battle took place in South Africa during the second half of the 20th century which was observed by most people all over the world who were interested in race relations.

Slavery in South Africa was abolished at the beginning of the 19th century, about fifty years before Lincoln freed the slaves in the USA in 1863. South Africa at that time was a British colony. The attitude of the British towards the African population was one of paternal tolerance with some degree of assistance, mostly in the field of education. Little was done to further their progress towards improving their social status or their evolution toward attaining voting rights. When South Africa became a dominion within the British Commonwealth the South African government continued to practice the same policies towards the native population as were practiced by Mother England. However, when the pro-British government of the Union of South Africa was defeated by the Nationalist Party (consisting mostly of the Afrikaner section of the white population) after World War II in the national elections of 1948 a change occurred in the status of the black people. Things became worse for them.

Some old laws which were not always seriously observed were re-enacted and were more forcibly carried out while new laws, even more stringent, were added. Black people were moved en masse to remote areas of the country which the authorities said was their homeland, families were separated, and some people who were considered white in the past were now re-classified as black because of some far distant ancestral inter-mixture. Marriage across the color bar was forbidden. Fraternization was disallowed; blacks and whites could not mingle on a social level. A White person was not allowed to entertain a Black friend in his home. Everybody carried an Identity Card with his race clearly marked. There were cases of brothers and sisters categorized under different racial groups. Those who appeared to be Black in a so-called

White family were forced to leave the home and school, and live in a structure in the back yard and go to a different school appropriate for his or her race.

The Job Reservation Act determined that Black people could only hold certain jobs which were considered to be suitable for them, and the Group Areas Act determined where they may reside. Certain areas of the country were named as Bantu Homelands, and all those who were born in a particular part of the country were told to return to their homeland and work there; they could not work outside that homeland, except with special permission which was difficult to attain. The only problem was that there was no work in the Homelands as there was almost no infrastructure, and industries had not been developed. Yet with no work available families needed to be supported.

Non-observance of the Pass Laws were responsible for crowding of the jails, as any non-white person found outside his home after a certain hour, without a note from his employer permitting him to be out on the streets, was imprisoned. A black man requiring a blood transfusion could only receive blood from a person designated as black; he could only be admitted to a hospital for black people. Park benches, queues at banks and other places, water fountains were designated as "For Whites only" or "For Blacks only". Movie theaters were for Whites only; Blacks had their own theaters where the authorities would allow them to see movies which were considered suitable for them; movies that might entice any racial, social or political unrest were forbidden.

The entire system of apartheid was explained by the ruling Nationalist Party as "separate, but equal". Obviously, the statement sounded as though all races were being treated on an equal basis, but it was anything but equal. White supremacy was being maintained while people of color were being held down. Even the blind could see who was boss.

The primary architect of the system of 'apartheid' (meaning 'apartness') was Dr. Hendrik Verwoerd, another one of those people who were originally aliens to the country in which they ruled. Verwoerd was born in the Netherlands. His family moved to South Africa while he was still a child. They later moved to Southern Rhodesia (Zimbabwe, today) where Hendrik received his education, and then at a later date came back to South Africa. For his further education he was offered scholarships to England, but he preferred to disregard these invitations; instead he went to Germany to study at their universities. He came home to South Africa prior to the commencement of the Hitler regime.

He originally studied theology as his father had been a minister of the Dutch Reformed Church, but he soon changed to psychology. He received a Ph. D. and started doing social work amongst poor South African Whites. He soon became editor of 'Die Transvaaler', a daily newspaper that supported the policies of the Nationalist Party which was basically anti-British. When the British Royal family toured South Africa he urged his readers not to pay any attention to their visit. He openly supported Germany during the Second World War, hoping for a Nazi victory. He objected to the entry of Jews who had been displaced and could be saved as a result of the Nazi outbursts upon them. Many of his Party members, including a future prime minister (John Vorster) and future Cabinet ministers, spent time in jail during World War II because of their seditious behavior and support for the enemy.

He soon entered into the political arena and was given the Cabinet post which included African education. He believed that their education should be strictly limited and not go beyond a certain point. It did not take a long time before he became the leader of the Nationalist Party and, later, Prime Minister of South Africa. Once Premier, he even more strongly enforced the apartheid policies. He quoted the Bible when discussing the Black population, likening them to 'the children of Ham' whom God had punished and described them as 'hewers of wood and drawers of water'. He delineated nine territories scattered all around the country which he declared to be Bantustans where those with ethnic connections to these territories were expected to live and work. These lands were supposed to develop into farming and industrial areas, but were slow in doing so because of poor soil quality and insufficient funds. South Africa, as a whole, was thriving through gold and diamond mining and industrialization but the homelands were stricken with few resources, poverty and an absence of development. This was supposed to be 'separate but equal'!

Dr. Verwoerd introduced a country-wide vote in 1961 asking the people (only whites were entitled to a vote) whether they would want to change the constitution to a Republic. He cited India as a republic within the British Commonwealth, and suggested that South Africa, too, could go that way. In order to ensure a vote in his favor he lowered the voting age and extended the vote to the Whites only of South-West Africa, which was a Mandated Territory of South Africa (granted by the League of Nations after World War I; today it is an independent country called Namibia). These people had never before voted in South African elections. However, a scant majority of the overall electorate voted yes. The British Commonwealth, at its next meeting, required South Africa to re-apply for membership. The non-white countries of the Commonwealth did not wish to accept South Africa as long as its laws of apartheid were in place; Canada argued in a similar way. Verwoerd withdrew his application, leaving South Africa as a republic outside the British Commonwealth. This made matters easier for him as he no longer had the members of the British Commonwealth Club looking over his shoulders and criticizing his actions.

Because of the repressive laws the Black population held a number of strikes against the administration. One of these occurred at Sharpeville outside a police station when a large number of demonstrators were killed. An era of sabotage and bombings followed in different areas, expressing the dissatisfaction of the Black populace.

There were two attempts on Dr. Verwoerd's life. He was first shot in the face at the Fairgrounds near Johannesburg, but survived the assault. However, he was less fortunate with the second assassination attempt when his killer, Dmitri Tsafendas, a staff member of the Parliament building, walked right up to Dr. Verwoerd one day during a Parliamentary session and stabbed him. Strangely, the killer gave his reason for the assassination of Verwoerd as being due to the fact that he was doing too much for the Blacks, a matter that the whole world would certainly question!

General Smuts

While on the subject of South Africa it is fitting to mention General Jan Christiaan Smuts. Here we have a South African who turned out to be more British than the British! He was a member of the Boer commandos during the Anglo-Boer War (1899 – 1902), leading many guerilla attacks upon the British forces in the Cape Province. He was one of the great Boer heroes of the country and was regarded as a thorn in the side of the forces that came from the entire British Empire. He led daring Boer commando raids deep into British–held territory where he and his men caused severe havoc, blowing up their weapon supplies and their bases.

However, in 1902, out of the blue, a news report arrived stating that a peace delegation from the Boers, which included General Smuts, arrived to meet with the British military leaders at a town called Vereeniging. The Boer forces were surprised and could not understand why this was being done. They were not losing the war; they had entered into a stalemate and wished to continue fighting. They felt that they were more than a match for the foreigners on their own soil, and they would soon drive them out. They knew the country far better than their enemy did. They could attack when least expected and disappear without being found – and they could continue doing this for a long time! So why was there a peace delegation? Yet peace was declared, and South Africa joined the British Empire, later receiving dominion status.

This premature peace treaty proved to be the stumbling block that split the White population into two – those that remained enemies of Britain despite the peace treaty and those that said "Let us forget the past, and let us join the British community of nations'.

Smuts who had been an arch-enemy of the British now became a loyal British subject. He became an Anglophile and fell in love with his enemy, while the majority of the Boer population vented their hate upon him for having 'jumped ship' and joined the hated British! Here was a South African-born leader who had become a friend of the enemy. He loved the British and they loved him. In fact, the British relied on him and he relied on them. In World War I he helped to drive the Germans out of German South-West Africa (after the war the League of Nations ceded it to South Africa as a mandated territory). When the Welsh coal strike during the middle of the war threatened to cripple the British war effort he went to meet with the leaders and the miners on their own territory, and broke the strike with his charisma, by just talking to them and getting them to sing patriotic songs for him! The next day the miners went back to work and the coal production continued unabated.

Leading up to World War II he was Prime Minister of South Africa. When the war broke out he found himself in the unenviable position of wanting to go to war on the side of Britain, but his fellow Afrikaners preferred to be on Germany's side. Germany had given them assistance during the Boer War, which was less than forty years before that, and many remembered those days well. They hated the British who had caused so much trouble in their land, and sent many of them into concentration camps where thousands had died. Only Germany had proved to be their friend.

Smuts had many of his fellow countrymen arrested and sent to jail because of their anti-British protests (as stated earlier in this chapter). Incidentally, some of these people became members of the apartheid government later after World War II. There might have been a civil war if he had committed South African forces entirely to Britain, so he cleverly declared that his troops would fight in Africa only in order to keep the continent free of Nazism. Thus South African troops fought in Africa clearing the Germans from Tanganyika (now Tanzania) and the Italians from Ethiopia, Somalia and Eritrea, and the Vichy French forces from Madagascar. Finally they ended up with the British forces in North Africa under General Montgomery. They fought at El Alamein, Tobruk and Sidi Rezegh. Despite the promise of fighting in Africa only, South African troops were sent to help conquer Italy after Africa was cleared of Italian and Nazi control.

Nevertheless, despite the limited role his forces played in the war Field Marshall Smuts (he received a promotion) was made a member of the British War Cabinet. He was in constant contact with Winston Churchill and other leaders of the British forces. Churchill trusted his opinion more than almost anyone else's. He was a powerful voice in British war policy.

However, at the conclusion of the war he had to contend with his own people at the General Election. By being such a great friend of Britain he dug his own grave. The Afrikaners decided that he must go, and he was defeated. The apartheid government took over. This was his payment for his pro-British stance. You will remember that Winston Churchill also underwent a similar fate after World War II when he was defeated by Clem Atlee's Labor Party.

During the Boer War Smuts had decided that it was pointless for his land to continue the struggle against the entire British Empire whose troops came pouring in daily. He realized that they could not defeat the British with their countless resources of men and materiel. This war could have gone on forever with loss of lives and hardships to his people, but he could never win. If you can't fight them, join them, he thought. So we see that enemies can become friends, and even staunch allies! He was involved in two world wars on Britain's side, and received many glowing awards for his endeavors. He could not have been a greater patriot had he been born an Englishman.

Sonia Gandhi

Sonia Gandhi was born in Italy, in the vicinity of Turin. Her name was Antonia Maino before she changed it. Her father served in the German army and fought on the Russian front in World War II. Her family supported Benito Mussolini. While studying at Cambridge in England she met Rajiv Gandhi, also a student. He was the son of Indira Gandhi who in turn was the daughter of Pandit Jawaharlal Nehru, the first Prime Minister of India following Indian independence in 1948. Sonia married Rajiv, and returned to live in India in the home of Indira, Rajiv's mother, while she was Prime Minister. Sonia played no part in politics; nor did she appear to be interested in it. She was a home-keeper and took care of her children.

While Indira was still Prime Minister she was assassinated. She was followed as Prime Minister, by her son, Rajiv. Strangely, he too was assassinated. Sonia was then offered the leadership of the government after her husband was killed. She did not feel adequate for this position, but she was becoming interested in politics at this time so she accepted the presidency of the Congress Party which was the governing Party of India. The Congress Party supplied most of the prime ministers of India since independence; it was and is the most important political force in the country considering that it formulates the policies of the Party, and it is the Congress Party that usually rules the country.

It is true that Sonia has never been the leader of India, but she has been offered the leadership position more than once, and has refused it. There would have been some controversy over the matter had she accepted the post. Many Indians would not have wanted an Italian woman to lead their country. However, she is more comfortable as the head of the Congress Party, because she holds the reins of government in her hands. As most of the prime ministers have been of that Party, it makes her position one of paramount importance. She is so intertwined with the affairs of India that her Italian heritage has been left far behind, making her more Indian than Italian. She is the longest serving President in the history of the Congress Party. She is considered to be one of the most influential and respected women in the world.

Golda Meir

Israel was declared an independent country in 1948. It was therefore impossible for the early prime ministers to have been born there since at the time of their births it did not exist. The early prime ministers actually came from Eastern Europe and were Ashkenazi Jews who settled in Palestine, which was the name of the British Mandate (originally named by the Romans) before a portion of it became Israel. They had all spent many years living in the Biblical home of the Jews, drawn there by a Biblical urge to return to the home of their ancestors or by anti-Semitism and pogroms in the lands in which they were born. Golda Meir (originally Mabovich) was born in Kiev (now the Ukraine) in 1898, but she re-located to the United States before she went to

Israel. By the time that she arrived in Israel she was already married. She became the first female prime minister of Israel.

Her father, a carpenter, had originally come to the US alone to seek work. When he found a job in Milwaukie he sent for his family in Kiev to come and join him. Golda was thus brought up and educated in Wisconsin. Contrary to her mother's desire that she leave school and get married she went to Denver, Colorado to live with her married sister. At their home she met people who had socialism and Zionism on their minds. She attended all their meetings and discussions. After returning to Milwaukie she became a school teacher and married Morris Meyerson (changed later to Meir) on condition that they would go and settle in Palestine, a country that they both had learnt to love even before they had arrived there. They moved there in 1921.

She commenced working on a kibbutz, picking fruits and almonds, but then she and her husband moved to Tel Aviv, and later to Jerusalem. She immediately became involved in political matters and joined different organizations until she was elected as a member of the Histadruth, the labor organization which was a part of the Jewish Agency. She and her children returned to the US on assignment for two years while her husband remained in Israel. From then on her relationship with her husband cooled off and they went their own separate ways until his death in 1951. She was present as a representative of the Jewish Agency at Evian in the south of France when the nations of the world met in 1938 in order to try to re-locate some of the Jews of Germany as Hitler's rantings against the Jews augured for a dismal future ahead for them in that country. At the meeting the US, Britain and other European countries would not agree to accept any Jews – only Trajillo of the Dominican Republic was prepared to take in 100,000 Jews. He needed their business acumen to improve the economy and he also hoped to lighten the skins of his people by dilution with 'white' Jewish blood, as most Dominicans had a dark skin complexion (while he was light-skinned). A mere 600 went there, and most re-located soon after. The Conference at Evian was an abysmal failure.

It fell to the office that Golda Meir held at the Jewish Agency to deal with the British administration of Palestine – a difficult position as Britain was not very friendly towards the Jews of Palestine at that time, restricting immigration and pretending to be even-handed with both Jews and Arabs. After the United Nations divided Palestine into a Jewish and Arab state she was a signatory to independence. When the British administration moved out Golda Meir dressed in the clothes of an Arab woman, and went to Jordan to speak to King Hussein, asking him not to invade Israel together with the other Arab states in the impending Arab invasion. He said "Don't declare independence so soon". She answered "We have waited two thousand years. Is that too soon?"

After the Six Day War she became ambassador to Moscow. It was important to get Stalin's friendship for the new State. Unfortunately, Stalin abhorred all forms of religion, and was not an easy convert for supporting a Jewish state. Later she served as Minister of Labor and also as Foreign Minister. When Levi Eshkol, the Prime Minister, died in office she was elected to be the next Prime Minister.

In 1972 at the Munich Olympics eleven members of the Israeli team were taken hostage and later assassinated by members of the Black September group of the PLO. This shocking incident had a profound effect on Israel and most of the world, and marred the rest of the Games. Golda Meir instructed the Mossad that she wanted the assassins to be hunted down and their lives ended. Over a period of a few years each one of the assassins was rooted out and killed in different parts of the world.

The Yom Kippur War of 1973 came as a big surprise and was a black mark in the history of Israel. Israel was not ready and did not suspect that the Arab nations were about to attack. Some rumors had reached Golda Meir that the Arabs were preparing, but her War Minister and other Cabinet members set no credence to these stories and disregarded them as just rumors. However, while most of the nation was praying at the synagogues on the holiest day of the year Syria attacked from the east and the Egyptians sent their tanks rolling through the Sinai Peninsula in the south. Israel was stunned for the first few days until she was able to recover her equilibrium from the shock. Then she sent the Arab armies sprawling, pushing the Syrians back to their own borders and re-establishing control of the Sinai Desert. Israeli forces were at the gates of Port Said and about to invade Egypt when President Nixon and Henry Kissinger, Secretary of State, forced them to retreat and threatened them with an arms embargo. Despite another Israeli victory in the Yom Kippur War there was great disappointment in Israel when they realized that they had been caught napping while their land was almost over-run. Who was to blame? Moshe Dayan who was in charge of the forces received a great deal of criticism, but so did Golda as this had occurred on her watch.

She resigned soon after the war, but she was always loved by her people. She had numerous admirers throughout the world. She was the first Israeli female prime minister and was looked upon as the mother of her people – a woman who was born in Kiev, brought up in America, and had never been to Israel until she was in her twenties, but once there she was as patriotic as anybody who was born in that land. In 1978 she died of cancer of her lymphatic system.

De Valera

In 1882 Eamon de Valera was born in New York City to an Irish couple who had left Ireland to make a new life in the New World. There is no evidence to prove that Juan Vivion de Valera was his true father or, indeed, whether his so-called parents were ever married as no certification has ever been found. However, when Juan Vivion died in 1885 the family was disrupted, and Eamon was sent to Limerick to be brought up by his grandmother. Even though his mother re-married the young boy was never re-invited to come back to her in New York City. He grew up and was educated in County Limerick. He wished to enter into the Catholic Church and serve God from within the Church, but the unclear history of who his father was would probably have caused problems with his entry or later promotions in the Church. Instead he became a school teacher.

His first involvement with Irish independence was by joining the Irish Volunteers who favored Home rule and were opposed to the Ulstermen in the north who favored remaining under British rule. He rose in status in his military group, and when the Easter Rebellion broke out in 1916 he found himself in charge of defending a section of Dublin. They proclaimed an Irish Republic, but were soon defeated, and most of the men were arrested and executed. Some have hailed him as a hero in the Easter Rebellion, whereas others have said that he lost his nerve and behaved in a bizarre manner.

De Valera was the only one who survived following the round-up after the rebellion because he was a US citizen and the US government pled for his life. When he was released from jail a few years later he was elected to the British parliament as an Irish representative probably as a result of the fact that most of the leaders had been executed. However, he refused to serve at Westminster. Instead he formed an independent parliament and was elected president. He separated from Sinn Fein, his original party, and started a new one (Fianna Fail). He broke with Michael Collins, the other prominent leader, because he disagreed with him on the partition of Ireland which Collins was prepared to accept.

In 1932 Fianna Fail won the election, and De Valera became in charge of the Dail (Irish parliament). Acts of guerilla warfare continued against the British. His goal was to keep the country close to Catholicism and to go back to the Gaelic past as well as to strengthen the bonds to the Gaelic language and placing it ahead of English. He was interested in democratic reform and in re-building derelict areas and bringing people back to agricultural living. Apart from Ulster the rest of Ireland (now called Eire) gained independence from Britain in 1937. In 1938 he was able to get the British who still occupied some Irish ports to withdraw and return the territory to Eire.

During World War II he decided to keep Eire neutral. There was little desire to fight with the British. If he had not remained neutral it is likely that Eire would have suffered damage from the German blitz. He received some very severe criticism when, at the end of the war, he commiserated with the German people at the news of the death of Adolf Hitler.

He was a dominant figure of world politics in the 20th century. He died in 1975, having been head of his country for 21 years and president for 14 years. He was a controversial figure throughout his life and an enemy of Great Britain; he also had enemies in Ireland. Yet he was an American of Irish descent who was not born in Ireland but had the tenacity to fight for an independent Ireland and to bring back the pride, style of living and language of the past. The British Isles was no longer one united country; Eire occupied a large portion of it.

Saladin

If we go back almost a thousand years into the history of the Middle East we will find that Saladin was once the Sultan of Egypt. He was born in 1137 in Tikrit, which is in present-day Iraq and also the birthplace of Saddam Hussein. He became the ruler of an Arab state, Egypt, but he was neither an Arab nor an Egyptian. He was a Kurd. In his early life he was more interested in religion than in warfare, but he joined the army and was soon elevated to higher commands.

He became a leader of the Syrian forces attacking Egypt. After victory was proclaimed he became the Sultan of Egypt. He used the finances from Egypt to invade and take over the rest of Syria and the neighboring lands. With the funds at his disposal he went on to conquer Northern Mesopotamia. In fact, he united the Muslim world from Egypt to Mesopotamia. Now he was able to go to war in the Holy Land against the Crusaders and drive them out of Jerusalem in 1187, bringing peace into the land called Palestine by the Romans. Ever since the Crusaders had taken over Jerusalem in 1099 there had been mass murder there from both sides.

Once Saladin was ensconced in Jerusalem the Crusaders could never get it back again. He drove them out of most of the Holy Land. Pope Gregory III then called for the Third Crusade. It was led by Richard the Lion-heart of England, Emperor Frederick Barbarossa of Germany and Philip II of France – a formidable group. They could not re-capture Jerusalem, although they did get some other parts of Palestine back. Amidst the battles taking place Richard the Lion-heart developed a fever. Saladin offered him the services of his own personal doctor and supplied him with fruit and water. The defeated Richard returned home and became King of England, never returning to the Middle East.

There was a reason for Saladin's offer of fruit and water to the enemy. This way he could send his spies in to the enemy camp to deliver the gift. Thereby they could learn how many men were involved in the fighting and notice the number of weapons that the enemy possessed. Saladin made a pact with the Crusaders allowing Westerners permission to visit the Holy Places. A fourth Crusade to re-take Jerusalem failed once again. He offered free passage to the Jews who wished to return to their Biblical home.

Saladin ruled over Egypt, Syria, Palestine, what is now called Iraq and most of the Middle East. His empire was known as the Ayyubid Dynasty (Ayyubid refers to Job, which was a part of his full name). He died in 1193, but the Ayyubid Dynasty continued into the middle of the 13th century when it was over-run by the Mamelukes.

So we see that in many cases aliens to a land may show even more patriotism, enthusiasm, ambition and strength than the natives themselves. This could not happen in the United States where a citizen must have been born within the country in order to serve as president. In fact, after President Obama was elected there was a group of Republicans who claimed that his birth certificate was a forgery and that he was not born in Hawaii, but in Indonesia. Of course, this was a nonsensical political maneuver to void his presidency which was quickly disproved and put to rest.

Bishop of Paris

We have discussed foreigners becoming heads of state or military leaders in the country of their adoption. Could you visualize a Jew becoming the Bishop of Paris and being suggested as a future Pope? Such is the life of Aaron Lustiger whose parents came from Poland and settled in Paris at the time of World War I. They were Ashkenazi Jews who had set up a retail store in Paris to provide for themselves and their two children. But after the outbreak of World War II and the Nazi occupation of Paris they moved to Orleans. They then moved further south to try and get away from the pro-Nazi Vichy government who had already demanded that all Jews wear yellow badges. They left their children temporarily in the care of a Catholic family for their protection while they attempted to escape to a safer area. The children were exposed to Catholicism in their new home, and so young Aaron soon opted for baptism, adding Jean-Marie to his name. He was followed by his younger sister who also became a Catholic.

In the meantime the mother went back to Paris and re-opened the store, but it was not long after that she was arrested and taken to Auschwitz where her life soon came to an end. When the Lustiger children were re-united with their father after the war he urged them to renounce their Catholicism. They refused to do so as it was the only faith with which they really knew, the only one with which they had had any contact. After the war Aaron went to the Sorbonne and later continued with his Catholic religious education at a Carmelite seminary. He received criticism from many quarters for his open display of Catholicism. His father was very upset about it, and so were many rabbis, including Rabbi Lau, Chief Rabbi in Israel. Aaron replied that he was a fulfilled Jew; he would always remain a Jew – just like Jesus and all the Apostles, none of whom renounced their Judaism. Judaism, he said, was meant to act as a light to all the 'goyim' (non-Jews). Christianity, he believed, was an offshoot of Judaism. This was similar to the belief of James, brother of Jesus, who was the leader of the early Christians in Jerusalem.

After Christ was crucified James took on the leadership of the new religion. Neither did he and his followers deny that they were Jews. Only after the Romans defeated the Jews round about 70 A.D. did Christianity in Palestine wither away. Christian leadership fell into the hands of Paul of Tarsus who separated himself from Judaism.

Lustiger believed in priestly celibacy, was against abortion and did not wish to see women in clerical appointments in the church. All people were created in the image of God, and were thus equal. Therefore he opposed racism and anti-Semitism. He was a strong supporter of Israel as a state, and visited it a few times. He was a good friend of Pope John Paul II; both his parents and John Paul came from Poland.

When the Vatican considered canonizing Queen Isabella of Spain he opposed such a move as she and King Ferdinand had expelled the Jews from Spain and had instituted the Inquisition in 1492. Pope John Paul appointed Aaron as Bishop of Orleans in 1979, and later, in 1981, as the Bishop of Paris. Lustiger acted often as adviser to John Paul and took some special trips with him. He was considered as a possible successor to John Paul after he would leave the scene. When a group of Carmelite nuns wanted to build a convent at a site at Auschwitz the Jews of the world resisted such a move as this was considered hallowed ground where countless Jews had been massacred by the Nazis, Aaron Lustiger joined in the resistance, and with John Paul's help such a move was prevented.

This is all very strange since for two thousand years the Catholic Church has been unfriendly to the Jews. In many lands the Jews had been persecuted by Catholicism. The Crusaders would kill Jews in Europe on their way to Jerusalem where they went to fight the Muslims in order to capture the Holy places. Jews were accused of killing Christian children for the purpose of making Passover matzos. Jews were considered to be responsible for poisoning the wells and causing outbreaks of bubonic plague. Jews were blamed for the crucifixion of Jesus. The Spanish Inquisition declared that all Jews were to convert to Catholicism or be exiled; those who remained and did not convert were to die. Two thousand years of Catholic anti-Semitism! And now a Jew was the Catholic Bishop of Paris! This was partially the work of John Paul who was dissatisfied with the state of Catholicism in Paris. Don't forget that it was also Pope John Paul who absolved the Jews for the killing of Christ which was supposed to put an end to a two thousand year accusation.

Lustiger was unlike most Bishops. He was often seen riding a moped; he smoked cigarettes. He attended the local synagogue to say 'kadish' (Jewish prayer for the dead) for his deceased mother. He said that he felt that upon the crucifix was attached a yellow star. He insisted that with his baptism he renounced nothing of Judaism; he only added to it.

When he died in 2006 his funeral service was held at Notre Dame Cathedral. President Sarkozy of France, who had been vacationing in the United States flew back for the services. Holy men from all over France and the Vatican and other lands were present. Rabbis, too, were present (the most orthodox would not enter a church). At the service Aaron's cousin intoned the Hebrew kadish, which must have been the first time that the Hebrew prayer for the dead was said at a funeral service in Notre Dame Cathedral.

It can be said with honesty that the leader of the Catholic Church in Paris was a Jewish Bishop.

CHAPTER 2

Unlikely Heroes

One cannot become a doctor or lawyer unless one trains for the profession. Likewise, we generally expect that leaders of armies had been soldiers in the past and had fought wars, rising in the ranks until finally reaching their positions of dominance. We also expect that heads of state would have gained their experience through the political arena. However, occasionally we meet up with unlikely heroes untrained in the field in which they have excelled.

Joan of Arc

Truth is stranger than fiction. Nobody would believe that a seventeen year –old girl could have lead the French army against mighty England - a girl not versed in warfare and never having wielded any weapons, but who had been talking to angels and dead saints! Does this sound credible? However, this is not a fairy tale, nor is it mythology. It is the story of Joan of Arc, and it is historically true.

The Hundred Years' War between England and France was taking place at that time. It lasted from 1337, and ended in 1443. The cause for this conflict started with the arrival of William the Conqueror in England in 1066. He was also the Duke of Normandy, so he brought a large part of French real estate (Normandy) with him to England. Later Henry II (great grandson of William) married Eleanor of Aquitaine, and when she died he inherited Aquitaine from her. When Philip VI of France, years later, demanded that the English kings pay feudal homage to him Edward III, the reigning English monarch, refused. Thereby Philip confiscated Aquitaine. Edward said that this could not be done as he was really the King of France as well as England since he was the closest living relative to the recently deceased King Charles IV; he was even closer to Charles than Philip was. Edward's father had married Isabelle, daughter of Phillip IV. In the face of these unreasonable demands and with his family kinship to the French royalty and the holding of these large areas of French real estate Edward felt justified in invading France.

England was a sparsely inhabited country at that time, and did not appear to be equal to the task of going to war with mighty France, but apparently the use of the longbow gave her an edge on the advancing French fighting forces because of its greater accuracy. The British conquered Normandy and, with ownership of Aquitaine which had increased in size, Britain was now in control of most of northern France. After Henry V of England became King of England he was about to announce himself as King of France at the time of the defeat of the French army at Agincourt in 1415, but the majority of the French refused to accept English domination.

Apart from the Hundred Years' War with England taking place at that time there was also a civil war occurring within France at the same time, between the Orleanists and the Burgundians. King Henry's British victory was accomplished with the help of the men from Burgundy. The Burgundians and the English had been firmly rooted together in the trading of cloth and wool. The English had only to defeat Orleans in order to take over the rest of France. These were dark days for the French nation.

Joan of Arc was born on January 6th, 1412 in the village of Domremy in Lorraine, which is in the eastern part of France. She came from a very religious family. When she was 12 years old she had visions and heard the voices of angels and other heavenly dwellers, including Archangel Michael, who had recently become the patron Saint of the French army. Many today would have diagnosed her as being epileptic (apparently she suffered from seizures) and/or schizophrenic with symptoms of visual and auditory hallucinations. She said that her visions were accompanied by bright lights and the ringing of bells (a familiar aura preceding epileptic seizures). Orleans became the focus of Joan's visions. Archangel Michael told her to drive the English and Burgundians out of Orleans because God supported Charles' claim to the throne. She tried to get to see Charles in order to give him that information, but she was not permitted to visit him and nobody would listen to her.

At this stage Orleans was under siege and Charles' army was in a very poor predicament. His mother sided with England, saying that Charles was illegitimate, and thus not the true heir to the throne. When it was discovered that Joan of Arc had correctly predicted the date of the defeat of Charles she was permitted to see him on her third attempt at trying to arrange a meeting. Charles had her checked by the priests. They said that there was 'nothing improper about her, only good; she displayed humility, chastity and piety, propriety and simplicity'.

She told Charles that he would be crowned as King of all of France at Reims and that Jesus was on his side. She also told him many things that made him sure that only a messenger of God could be privy to such secrets. Therefore she was named by Charles as the leader of the army against the advice of many of his commanders. She was dressed as a man so as to prevent rape by the troops, even though this was attempted on more than one occasion, even by a duke. She declared herself a virgin, and would only sacrifice her virginity on God's command. She called herself La Purelle – the Virgin – and said that she was sent in the name of God and that Jesus supported her in what she was doing. Charles was delighted to submit to her leadership.

She reformed the troops. She put an end to swearing and drove out the prostitutes from the camps. She stopped all looting and abuse of civilians. She instituted confessions, and allowed men who had run away to confess and return to duty. She had a volatile temper, slapping those who were rude to her or did not participate in prayer and confession. She herself did not fight and carried no weapons, but she always accompanied her troops.

"England, go back to England, or I will drive you out of France" she called. She brought the army to besieged Orleans, leading her troops and encouraging them while carrying a banner. She held no arms or bow and arrows. She said that she did not wish to kill or harm anyone. Yet she was exposed to the same dangers as the rest of her troops. When she was hit by an arrow she went ahead into battle as though nothing had happened. Nevertheless when she saw that her troops were losing morale she acted as their cheer-leader. Yet she and her men went on fighting until victory was in their hands. The English were driven back, and those who remained surrendered. She told Charles to go to Reims where he would be crowned Charles VII. Charles told everyone involved to get all military advice from Joan and to believe in her.

Joan pursued the retreating English engaging them in battle after battle until she arrived at Reims, where Charles was anointed Dauphin. She then wrote to the Duke of Burgundy, telling him to join Charles against the English.

She was again hit by a dart and, against her will, was not allowed to continue. The army became discouraged at that point and became disintegrated. The Royal Court would not give her permission to continue the war into Normandy. She defied the court and went into battle without permission. Her biggest fears were capture and betrayal. She sensed that she would be captured in this last battle.

In 1430 she was ambushed by the Burgundians. She refused to surrender, and had to be dragged off her horse. Charles tried to get her back from the Burgundians, but failed. Ransom was refused. Attempts at kidnapping her failed. After holding her as prisoner for four months she was handed over to the English. They were overjoyed. They had never feared an enemy commander as they had feared her. They held a trial for the purpose of revenge rather than for heresy. She was her own witness – she allowed no other. When she wished to appeal to the Pope it was disallowed. Many considered the tribunal illegitimate. They accused her of witchcraft, saying her banner had magical powers. They complained about her cross-dressing and the saints and demons that she had consulted. She was given a dress to wear, whereupon she had to deal with attempted rape on a number of occasions.

This peasant girl was nineteen years old at her execution; she was burned at the stake. She forgave her accusers and asked them to pray for her. She listened to the sermon. She was then tied to a tall pillar while she was openly sobbing. The flames rose, and she cried to Jesus, asking him and the saints of Paradise for assistance. Then her head dropped and she was dead.

Thereafter the war fizzled out as the British realized that the war was not getting them anywhere and that final victory after a hundred years did not appear to be forthcoming.

Thirty years later Joan of Arc received a posthumous acquittal. It was said that she had been convicted illegally without basis by a corrupt court operating in a spirit of manifest malice against Roman Catholicism. She was a martyr. She was beatified in 1909 and canonized in 1920. She had been a most unlikely heroine of France against its long-term enemy – England. Where else, apart from fairy tales and cartoons, have you heard of a woman – nay, a young girl – untrained in war, leading an army into battle and scoring so many victories while being cheered on by a king and his advisers? She achieved what no French commander before her was able to accomplish.

Lech Walesa

Another unlikely leader was Lech Walesa. Born in 1943 in Popowa, Poland, he was the son of a carpenter who was arrested by the Nazis before Lech was born and spent years in a concentration camp. Arriving home after the war, he never recovered and died from exhaustion two months later. Lech received a minimal elementary school education, and then became an electrician. The next few years were spent working as a car mechanic and doing military service, after which he went off to work in the Gdansk shipyards, also known as the Lenin Shipyards. Poland was a part of the Soviet Bloc, where the government was communist and under strict Soviet control.

He married, and had eight children. He was a religious Catholic. From the beginning his concerns were always with workers rights. When the workers at the shipyards went on strike because of higher food prices he was right behind them. Strikes were illegal, but that did not stop Walesa and the shipyard workers. When 30 people were killed by the authorities during the strikes he became more convinced that opposition to the government was essential. He was frequently laid off and sometimes arrested. He even lost his job, but when a fresh strike began he scaled the shipyard fence to join the workers and was immediately proclaimed leader.

Surprisingly and unexpectedly the president and the Soviet authorities gave permission for the shipyard people to strike when they deemed it necessary and allowed them the right to form a movement. Out of this proclamation the Solidarity movement was started in 1980 and soon grew to a total of 10 million members, obviously including numerous members from outside the shipyard. When matters worsened by 1982 martial law was introduced and many including Walesa were arrested and Solidarity was outlawed.

He was awarded the Nobel Peace Prize in 1983. His wife went to receive it for him as he was in jail. In 1989 Solidarity was re-instated. At the elections held soon thereafter Solidarity swept to victory. It was Walesa's Party that won, but he did not compete in the elections. Somebody else became the first Solidarity President.

However, at the next election he was a candidate, and was chosen as President. He introduced a free market economy. He asked for the removal of Soviet forces from Polish soil which was complied with, and he reduced the Polish debt. He moved in the direction of joining the European Union and NATO.

Yet there were complaints about him as President. It was said that he was too plain-spoken, he was insufficiently educated and too undignified. He was very rude to his competitors during the debates. He had argued with other Solidarity leaders who either left him or he excluded them, and was thus left with only a weak Solidarity core in his administration. He was a poor debater and his comments were often rough and crude. His popular support dwindled, and although he ran again for President he was never re-elected.

He voiced surprising opinions, such as stating that African countries needed Communism in order to advance; yet he had fought communism in his own land. It was alleged that he was a collaborator with the Secret Police under the Communist regime. He denied this, and the court accepted his story, but later other evidence was found stating that he gave the Secret Police information in exchange for money. Unfortunately, government files had been destroyed while he was President. This leaves the truth undecided.

Despite the bad reports about him after his leadership there is no question about it that he was a force for the good. In the dark days of Communism in Poland he risked his life to keep the torch of the Solidarity movement burning. His name and his presence allowed the movement to increase in strength. Because of him Solidarity membership multiplied. Solidarity was the greatest counter-force facing the Soviet Union from within its own Bloc. It was he that had asked the Soviets to withdraw from his country – and they did so! This action was one of a multiple of reasons for the collapse of the Soviet Union and Communism in Eastern Europe.

Nelson Mandela

Another unlikely hero came from South Africa. Who would ever have believed in the days of apartheid and white racism in South Africa that a black 'trouble-maker and upstart' who opposed the government and was sent to jail for life imprisonment would one day walk out of jail and become president of that country? Another fairy tale with a happy ending, you might say. It is the story of Nelson Mandela, who became a leader in a land where he – as well as the entire Black population - had been treated as a lower form of life, not deserving of a vote or many of the amenities enjoyed by the privileged white section of the population. Whoever would have thought that such an enemy of the people who was lucky to have escaped a death sentence would one day walk out of jail and rule over his jailers and, indeed, the entire country – and also become an idol of strength, justice and peace to the rest of the world?

Nelson was born in the section of the Cape Province in South Africa, known as the Transkei. His family was of royal blood, yet his father was defrocked by a white magistrate for not obeying orders. Thereupon he left town with his four wives and all his children, and moved to Qunu, a neighboring town.

Years to come when Nelson's father was about to die he asked the Regent to take care of his son, Nelson, whom he thought had a special capacity for learning. The Regent sent Nelson to the best schools that were available for black people. He ended up at Fort Hare, a British-style University for Black students. Here he received a sound education and proved to be a good student. When Nelson came home from University he found that the Regent had arranged a marriage for him. Nelson did not wish to marry this woman, so he fled – together with the Regent's son for whom similar arrangements had been made - to the gold mines in Johannesburg.

For the first time in his life he was now in a city run by White men, unlike the tribal lands where he had been brought up. Johannesburg was the center of the gold mining industry, and Nelson found himself as a security agent on a mine. However, when the authorities discovered that he was a fugitive from the Transkei they fired him. Again he disappeared, finding himself working as a clerk in a legal firm and taking courses at the University of the Witwatersrand. This was a very liberal school, and his fertile mind absorbed all the ideas and thoughts that he heard from students and teachers in the class-room and on the campus. In his spare time he became a boxer which kept him fit and was an outlet to some of his pent-up emotions that were brewing inside of him.

At this time he started going to political meetings, and met with some of the most important liberal political figures in the country as well as with the leaders of the African National Congress. He soon became a member of this organization.

He married and had two children with Evelyn. When they first married she thought that her husband was on his way to becoming a lawyer, but she soon saw that politics was overtaking his interest in legal studies. She was apolitical. He spent much time away from home with his political activities until one day he came home to find that she had taken the children and her belongings and had left him.

While at first he believed in passive resistance against the government in the manner of Gandhi, he soon changed his mind saying that the tyrannical leadership of the country could only be removed physically.

Gandhi had formulated his policies of passive resistance in South Africa before returning to India. Mandela proceeded to form and develop the military wing of the ANC – Umkhonto we Sizwe, translated in English as the Spear of the Nation – which was soon to be responsible for acts of terrorism against the regime. He said that it was ludicrous to attempt to fight the physical force used by the government with passive resistance. It was a matter of submit or fight, and he was not going to submit!

He spent time in jail for his anti-government activities. While out of jail he was frequently hiding from the police as he became known as a trouble-maker. He grew a beard and wore overalls representing different trades to disguise his identity. He even left the country illegally travelling to African and Middle Eastern countries where his men were being trained in the art of guerilla warfare. However, when he returned his car was spotted at the airport. He then became careless on many occasions when he could have been more meticulous about hiding his identity, and was finally captured in Natal. This invoked a five year sentence. His carelessness might have been because he wanted to get caught since a life underground did not give him an opportunity to confront the authorities. As a member of a banned party he did not have a platform, but in court he would be able to speak in his own defense. He needed to have his say. Court would be the only place where he could announce his views and talk against the government since the law would not allow the media to quote an enemy of the regime. Such people were considered as non-existent.

The Rivonia Trial was his undoing. Rivonia is a suburb outside Johannesburg. The ANC had its secret headquarters in a house in this suburb, and while he was in hiding Mandela had spent much time in Rivonia. When the police got wind of it they raided the premises and found many secret and treasonous documents, a number of which involved Mandela. He was brought back to trial, and received a life sentence for attempting to overthrow the government. At this trial he saw that he had a platform, and he used it to expose his views, his opinions of the white racist government and his ideas for the future. He and many other members of the ANC spent about twenty-five years as political prisoners on Robben Island, a small off-shore island off Cape Town in the shark-infested South Atlantic Ocean.

In jail he demanded to be treated with respect by his jailers. Black prisoners were ordered to wear short pants. He preferred to wear long trousers, feeling that short pants for prisoners were chosen by the authorities in order that they should be made to look and feel like 'boys', and be made to appear more vulnerable. He demanded the right to wear long pants and to be treated decently. He achieved his demands. He encouraged his political prison-mates not to waste their lives in jail but to improve their education by applying for educational correspondence courses, which many of them did. This was sometimes known as the Robben Island College in jest since so many of these political prisoners received most of their education here by such means. Many members of Mandela's first government which followed the end of the apartheid regime had been co-prisoners on Robben Island and received their education from the correspondence courses in which they had enrolled.

The African National Congress was banned in South Africa. Its headquarters were in London. They were also functioning in Northern Rhodesia (now Zambia). The Robben Island prisoners had no way of keeping in touch with the leaders running operations for the ANC from abroad, so one of them who had an ability of producing script in tiny letters (he could write a whole page on a piece of paper the size of a stamp) would write messages on small scraps of paper which would be crumbled up and thrown over a specified fence where they would be picked up by a pre-arranged person and sent to ANC agents.

Mandela had married a second time. This time it was Winnie with whom he also had children. While he spent all those years in jail she kept the cause of the ANC going, since most of the leaders were either in jail or out of the country or in hiding. Winnie spent much time in prison as well, but she was not afraid to speak out whenever she had the opportunity. She visited Nelson whenever she was allowed to do so, but for a long time hers was the lone voice for her Party. Her role in keeping the ANC alive in those dark days should not be lost sight of. However, there was another side to Winnie. She had a soccer team, and unfortunately, she used her soccer team for purposes other than playing soccer – she used them to eliminate some of her enemies. She actually became an embarrassment to Mandela. Late in life he divorced her and married the widow of the president of Mozambique who had been killed in a suspicious air crash.

The Afrikaners who had ruled the land were a religious people who believed that the Blacks were the Children of Ham (Ham was the son of Noah) who were cursed by God to be 'hewers of wood and drawers of water'. They were only meant to work for the Whites, according to the ruling authorities; they were like children, (they said) lazy, untrustworthy and incapable of leading and would certainly never be capable of voting. (Even Abraham Lincoln, who freed the slaves in the United States, said that they should be free but were incapable of voting). There was no hope for the Blacks in South Africa to escape from their lowly position. Any attempt at improving their status would inevitably land the activists, White or Black, in jail.

The African National Congress in its fight for equality was considered tainted because they had had meetings with the Communist Party. Remember this was at the time of the Cold War. Communism was feared, and the South African Communist Party had been banned. You need not look further than the Un-American Activities trials in the United States conducted in the Senate by Joe McCarthy where so many intellectuals were disgraced because of alleged pro-Communist activities.

In fact, even though there were boycotts and sanctions against South Africa for its apartheid laws Britain and the US supported South Africa as a bastion against communism in Africa, and feared that the ANC would allow the USSR to make inroads into Africa. Truthfully the ANC was not communist. Mandela had said that in order to bring the South African government down help was needed, and he would accept help from anyone, communists included. In later years he was asked why he had hugged Arafat, embraced Qadaffi and shaken hands with Castro. He said 'Where were you, Britain and the US, when I needed help? You supported my enemy – the apartheid government - while Arafat, Qadaffi and Castro supported me! Do you want me to discard my friends who had helped me at the time of my greatest need?'

Over a period of twenty-five years times change and people change. Sanctions had a toll on the South African economy, sports, arts and culture. International sport boycotted South African teams. This hurt the country as South Africans love their sports. Visiting artistes would not tour the country – culture suffered as a result of an absence of fresh interventions. Foreign businesses were pulling out of the land and some local businesses were leaving, too. South Africa was becoming the pariah amongst nations. Also at this time the religious Afrikaner parents who felt that they had a mission to keep the Children of Ham (the Black people) in their place and not allow them any further rights were dying and being replaced by their university-educated children who were brought up in a more modern world and were of the opinion that all people deserved the right to vote. Pressure on the apartheid government was strengthening. Nations of the world witnessed the events in South Africa and were incensed at the inequality of the races. Almost all African countries had shaken off the bonds of colonialism. The writing was on the wall. Mandela who had been only asking for equal rights, which seemed logical enough, was still sitting in jail after more than twenty years. "Free Mandela" was being called out from all corners of the earth. Pressure on the apartheid government was increasing. One small country could not fight against the world.

The government had to bend. They said that they would free Mandela if he renounced violence. He said he would not renounce violence unless the government did the same. Dignitaries from other lands who wanted to meet with him had never been allowed to visit him. Now the government began to have a change of heart, and permitted such meetings. He was removed from Robben Island and placed in a prison near Cape Town, where conditions were much improved, for easy access. Tailors were sent to measure him for suits. He was given his own chef. He was not treated as a prisoner any more. Leading officials from overseas were allowed the opportunity to see him and talk to him. He was taken out for drives sanctioned by the government. Prison life, as he had experienced it, no longer existed. His confinement became more luxurious. Cabinet ministers came to talk to him. He was given respect. Even his jailers admired him for his dignity and his strength of spirit.

The rest is history. He was freed. The most despised man in the country, as far as Whites were concerned, became loved, pitied, respected and hailed as a hero – even by Whites! Elections were held, and this time it was one man, one vote. The whole country voted, not only the privileged 20% of the population that had always voted in the past. It was the first election in South Africa where the Blacks were allowed to vote. They stood in long lines to enjoy that moment of freedom where they now could do what they had never done before. They voted just like the rest of the civilized world! Mandela was elected by a landslide.

Of all the leaders of the world Mandela was probably the most loved and respected. Like Lincoln he made friends with his enemies. He did not go out to get vengeance from those who had subjugated him and held him down. He made friends with his jailers and members of the government that had despised him. Dr. Hendrik Verwoerd, who was once Prime Minister, was the architect of apartheid. It was his laws that placed the Black people in a sub-human situation. It was his laws that Mandela had been fighting and that had put Mandela in jail. Dr. Verwoerd was assassinated in Parliament many years prior to Mandela's release, but when Mandela became President, he went to visit his widow in her own home. Even though Verwoerd had been his enemy he still treated him and his widow with respect! He did not appear to harbor feelings of revenge.

The South African rugby team was adored and cheered by the Whites, but hated and booed by the Blacks. When he became President the South African team played New Zealand for the world championship. The Blacks were about to come out to boo the South Africans and cheer the visiting team, as they had always done. Mandela, wearing the green South African rugby jersey was out there encouraging Black South Africans to cheer their team, which many did; and they won! He developed a relationship with the captain of the rugby team, who was an Afrikaner. The captain asked Mandela to be godfather to his two children.

He was a most unusual man. From being one of the most hated people in South Africa at the time of the Rivonia Trial he turned out to be one of the most loved people in the world. At the time of the Trial he was considered to be a trouble-maker. He used the trial as a platform to spread his message. Under any other circumstance his voice would never have been heard. At that time who would have listened to a Black man ranting and raving against the existing government? Any such person would have been arrested. He bided his time. He spent a quarter of a century in jail. He stood up against a powerful well-armed government that in the end realized that they had been beaten by one man! They were not beaten by his power, but by his ideas and his dedication to them!

He forgave his enemies. He respected all people. He went from the lower caste of society to prisoner to President. Until his death – and even since then - he has been idolized by the entire world. His life was not in vain - an unlikely hero. Truth is stranger than fiction!

Morris Cohen

Another unlikely hero is Morris Abraham Cohen. You have probably never heard of him and you might never hear of him again. But his life story deserves to be repeated. He was born in Poland in 1887 – that makes him the second person after Lech Walesa in this chapter from Poland. At the age of two his parents and all their children escaped from anti-Semitism and the pogroms in Poland and managed to arrive in England. Young Morris was brought up in the East End of London where he had a tough upbringing on the streets. He took up boxing as a sport, but also became a pickpocket. This soon landed him in jail and eventually he was sent to reform school. He lived the life of a character of Charles Dickens. His parents finally sent him to people that they knew in Saskatchewan in Western Canada, thinking that an agrarian life might improve his attitude towards cleaner living. The streets of London's East End were certainly not conducive to a more fruitful life for him.

The farming life in Saskatchewan did not suit him either. He ran away from his job and joined a carnival. He became a con man and continued with his behavior that he learnt on the streets of the East End of London. Soon he was arrested again for his irregular practices. One day he was at a Chinese restaurant and saw the Chinese owner being robbed. He attacked the robber, beat him up and threw him out on to the street. This action brought great praise from the Chinese people at the restaurant and in the surrounding area. No white person had ever fought for and protected any member of the Chinese community in Saskatchewan in the past. There were many Chinese in Canada at that time as they had been building the trans-continental rail-road, and many opted for remaining in America. This was a time when Asians were not very popular in Western Canada.

Morris Cohen, having proved himself to be a good fighter and friendly to the Chinese community was welcomed into a secret society that was supporting the new Chinese president Sun Yat Sen. Sun Yat Sen had defeated and overthrown the last of the emperors of the Qing dynasty. Cohen became an active member of this secret group, and developed a love for Chinese food and the Chinese people and their philosophy. He helped to collect funds in order to buy arms for Sun Yat Sen's army. Thus he became a friend of the Chinese people, and they trusted him.

He joined the Canadian forces in World War I, and after his return from Europe he decided to go to work in China. His plan was to work on the railroad, but having met certain officers of the army through the secret society in Saskatchewan he soon found himself as being in charge of Sun Yat Sen's bodyguard. He was called Ma Kun in China, which was as close as they could get to his name; it means 'clenched fist'. After receiving a bullet wound in his hand while protecting Sun Yat Sen during an assassination attempt he decided to carry two hand guns. He then became known as Two Gun Cohen. He was promoted to the rank of General in the Chinese army. Having fought in World War I and with his experience in boxing and his sense of dedication to the Chinese peoplehe was able to contribute much in the training of new soldiers for the Chinese army.

After Sun Yat Sen died he was followed by General Chiang Kai-Shek. Cohen continued working for Chiang. He remained as a general in the Chinese army – not only was he the only Jew, he was also the only non-Chinese in the Chinese army. Following the Pearl Harbor attack on the U.S., Japanese forces stormed through China. Sun Yat Sen's widow found herself holed up in Hong Kong. Cohen made plans for the evacuation of Sun Yat Sen's wife from Hong Kong on the last plane to leave the island, thus probably saving her life. Later, the widow of Sun Yat Sen became a member of the Communist Party and held some high positions in the administration.

He fought against the Japanese invaders, and was held captive and tortured by them. He returned to Canada following World War II. Unable to sit still he helped collect arms and deliver them to the Jews in Palestine who were intent to set up a Jewish state as promised by the Balfour Declaration in the wake of World War I. The survivors of the Holocaust needed a home, making a Jewish state even more imperative.

When the United Nations Security Council was about to discuss the partition of Palestine as a home for Jews and Arabs, it was known that China would vote against it. One dissenting vote on the Security Council would put an end to the dream of a Jewish state. Morris Cohen could not accept such a situation so he went to San Francisco where the United Nations was sitting prior to the construction of their headquarters in New York. He went to speak to the Chinese representative of the United Nations and asked him not to oppose the formation of a Jewish state. With him he brought a letter written by Sun Yat Sen before his death which he had kept, and showed it to the Chinese UN representative. The letter stated that the Jews deserved a home after all the suffering that they had gone through throughout history. China abstained from the vote, allowing the Security Council to pass the resolution and hand it down to the General Assembly where it, too, passed.

It could be said that Morris Cohen's intervention made a huge difference. If China had vetoed the resolution it would not have even gone to the General Assembly, and maybe there would no Israel today. The spirit and initiative of one man can build a nation! Ask Mandela!

He returned to live with his widowed sister in England, surrounded by family. He took a final trip to China which was now under a Communist administration. He was the guest of Prime Minister Chou En-Lai. He died in 1970 and was buried in Manchester, England. His tombstone is written in English, Hebrew and Chinese, and was donated by the widow of Sun Yat Sen, whose life he had saved.

Morris Cohen had little education and fell fowl of the law in his youth. His life was pointed in the direction of crime alternating with periods in jail. But he had a spark for life and was a colorful adventurer. He went wherever his urge sent him. He took advantage of a turn of events which led him into the revolutionary days of China after their imperial dynasties fell and he was a catalyst in the formation of the State of Israel!

He followed his heart. He was not afraid to stand up for what he believed.

Dimitar Peshev

Bulgaria, accompanied by the other Balkan States went to war against the Ottoman Empire in 1912-1913 in order to gain their independence. This was the First Balkan War in which they succeeded in ousting the Ottomans from their lands. The Balkan states divided the Balkans up between themselves. However, later in 1913 Bulgaria decided to go to war against Greece and Serbia, her former allies in the previous war, because she felt cheated by the territory which she had been given; she felt that she deserved more land than was meted out to her. As a result of the war she lost more territory. World War I soon broke out, and Bulgaria joined sides with Germany and the Austro-Hungarian Empire so as to re-claim the territory that she had wanted. Who else, but the winners of the war, were able to help her? Unfortunately she backed the wrong horse because Germany and Austro-Hungary lost the war.

In World War II, before attacking the Soviet Union Hitler bombed Belgrade and he and his allies invaded the Balkans. Bulgaria joined the Axis powers because Hitler promised that he would bring back to them the land which they had been claiming for the last twenty-five years. In fact, he handed over Macedonia and Thrace to Bulgaria for them to govern in the interim until final arrangements after the war would confirm the transfer.

King Boris III of Bulgaria was of German extraction. He started instituting Nazi anti-Jewish laws into his administration, such as Jews were prevented from marrying non-Jews and they were not allowed to move too far around the country; they wore symbols to identify them as Jews and all Slavic names amongst Jews were to be altered; they were not allowed to vote and had to pay a one-time tax amounting to 20% of their assets.

Hitler called for the Jews from Thrace and Macedonia (territories under Bulgarian jurisdiction), and about eleven thousand were sent to Treblinka where they all lost their lives. This was done with the help of Belev, a fiercely anti-Semitic parliamentarian, who made sure that everyone of them would be rounded up. Then Hitler called for the Jews of Bulgaria to be gathered up and sent north on the first stage to their final destination, most likely Treblinka.

When Dimitar Peshev heard about this he set about putting an end to such a move. He was not a Jew but had Jewish friends, one of which had told him that he had heard a rumor that the Jews were going to be sent out of the country. He was a member of the Bulgarian Parliament, an honest man and a human rights advocate. He was also deputy speaker of the House. He approached other parliamentarians and got the signatures of many to stop the wholesale transportation of Jews out of the country. He had difficulty in getting a meeting with King Boris, and when he finally did he stated his case that the King need not pander to all Hitler's wishes, especially if they were genocidal and unethical. At the same time the Orthodox Bishops said that they were opening their churches to save and protect Jews. Peshev said that the Jews had been in Bulgaria since before Byzantine times and were an integral part of the population. They had stood by and with the people throughout the entire history of the country, including the Ottoman rule. The bulk of the people clamored to let the Jews stay. It has not occurred often in history when a majority of the population were in favor of the Jews remaining. Some parliamentarians threatened to lie across the railway tracks, and if the trains transporting Jews wanted to go north they would first have to go over their bodies.

Peshev was fired from his position as deputy speaker, but the King softened to the wishes of his people. King Boris told Hitler that he needed the Jews to do some very heavy labor at the present time, but he would send them at a later date when their work was over. Hitler accepted that excuse.

The Jews of Bulgaria were sent to labor camps within the country where they lived under decent conditions, but they were never sent out of Bulgaria. Fifty thousand Jewish lives were saved. When they went home after the war they found their homes in good condition as the non-Jewish citizens had taken care of their properties in their absence. After the war most of the Bulgarian Jews immigrated to Israel, leaving a mere handful behind.

Peshev has been recognized at Yad Vashem (the Holocaust Memorial Museum in Jerusalem) as a Righteous Member among Nations who had assisted and saved Jews during World War II. Israel also set up a memorial statue for King Boris, but it has been removed since then because there were complaints about him for having allowed the Jews of Thrace and Macedonia to have been sent to Treblinka to their deaths.

There are some people who will rise to the top despite tremendous odds. When challenged they will not take no for an answer. They are simple and ordinary people who are driven by an idea or truth or justice. They are unlikely heroes.

CHAPTER 3

Unforgettable Characters

They seem to be like anybody else. They are not better or worse, or more intelligent or more stupid than the average person. Neither are they more boastful or more self-effacing than other people. They are just different, which makes them unforgettable. They have been cast in an unusual mold and do not conform to the common pattern.

Jack

On a lazy Sunday afternoon the phone rang. I picked up the phone. The voice at the other end asked in a slurred speech if he could speak to me, mentioning my name. I could hardly hear what he was saying as he was eliding his words making it difficult to understand him, but I did not hang up as I thought it might be an important call.

"Who is it?" I asked. He mumbled something back and I asked him to repeat what he was saying and to tell me his name. I did so a few times until I was able to finally recognize that he said that he was Jack, someone I had known very well - a great friend in the past, but I had not heard from for at least twenty years. His voice certainly never sounded like that in the past. I knew him as a tall, large figure, at least 6' 4" in height, strong, well-spoken and a lawyer by profession. The voice I was hearing now was somewhat familiar, but it sounded as though he might have had a stroke or some other catastrophe.

After enquiring into each other's health he said that he had arrived in Florida for a short vacation; he would like to meet me and that we should have lunch together. I agreed, and he added that he would bring his nurse to the phone to make arrangements. When I found out from her where they were living I chose a place that would be about equidistant from both of our residences, and suggested a time.

At the appointed time I awaited my friend in front of the restaurant that I had chosen. After about a half an hour of standing and walking around in circles I decided that he was probably not coming – either he could not find the place or perhaps something unforeseen had occurred. As I started walking back to my car a young woman hurriedly approached me and asked if I was Sidney. She said that she was Jack's nurse; she was sorry they were late, but it had taken longer than expected to get him prepared. However, they were now getting him out of the car. I walked with her to the car, and I saw three pretty young women helping Jack out of the car and placing him in a wheel-chair; no mean feat as he was still a very large and heavy man, despite his obvious deterioration in health. It appeared as though he had no or little use of his extremities and seemed bewildered. We greeted each other like long-lost brothers, and then in single file we all proceeded to the restaurant, got seated, and started talking.

It appears as though three months prior to our meeting on this day, Jack fell in the spa at his home, injured his head and became unconscious. He was taken to the hospital where he underwent surgery for bleeding within the skull. He was comatose for about three weeks, but when he recovered he was left with an inability to use his arms and legs and to speak clearly; he had no mental impairment, although he had certainly slowed down. He ate well, but had to be fed. The three nurses ate with us, and there seemed to be a fine camaraderie between all four of them. Apparently at his home on Long Island, New York they worked different shifts for him, one at a time while alternating with their work at the local hospital. Since the main period of his rehabilitation was now over Jack decided to take a short trip and vacation to Florida with his three lady-friend helpers.

With the assistance of his nurses who understood his speech far better than I did we caught up with some of the events of both of our lives in the past twenty years, as well as many memories from the past that we shared. We had been close friends and there was no good reason for us to have discontinued our friendship. It was probably because my first wife had died. Her friendship with Jack had pre-dated our marriage by a number of years, and she had been the glue that forged our relationship with Jack and his wife. After she died our friendship drifted apart mainly because the glue was no longer there and the communication just slipped away.

However, the luncheon was an enjoyable get-together, and it ended as abruptly as it had started. I do not know if I shall ever see him again. We said good-bye, and like many things in life the curtain came down on one more event!

Jack was a curt and acerbic man to many who knew him. He was a controversial person and was disliked by many people. He appeared to be as hard as nails. He did not partake in platitudes or engage in petty conversation in order to make people like him; his comments were often rude, short and biting. Yet to his family and friends whom he liked he was a totally different person. To them his hard exterior was not matched by his interior, which was soft and tender. He was a self-made man who had accumulated a large fortune in the real estate business in Manhattan. He owned many hotels and apartment buildings, and was always maneuvering to make a better deal. To those who knew him in the business world or in the legal profession he is remembered as a tough negotiator who did not give 'an inch', but those who knew him socially saw him as a kindly old teddy-bear always ready to give a helping hand to a person in need.

Despite his wealth he was his own handyman, plumber and electrician in all the properties that he owned, except when the problems were larger than he could handle. He would maintain all the air conditioners and boilers in his own buildings, thus saving expenses for repairmen. He knew where to get replacement parts cheaper, and he employed a small staff to do some of the more strenuous work. After working in the basement on the heating system for some hours he would come upstairs, and if there was a tenant who was behind with his rent he had no compunction to grab his clothing and personal belongings and throw them out through the front door followed by the tenant himself.

Such was the hard prickly covering to this man, similar to a cactus. But the cactus also has a soft juicy inside. I remember a young woman whom he knew only superficially. He had no sexual desires for her nor any particular interest in her, but when he heard that she had some form of cancer which was deemed to be incurable he was sorely affected by her condition. He came to visit her every Tuesday night, bringing her dinner and presents. He played scrabble with her and watched movies with her until the day that she died – and on that day he cried like a baby and did not go to work.

In the winters he and his wife and two children came to visit us almost every Sunday, and we had dinner together, while his and our children played together. In the summers we often went to his second home at Long Beach, Long Island. We would spend our days on the beach, and then return to his house, and eat and talk deep into the night.

I remember at least two occasions in which he helped us out. On one occasion while I was at work one day a man arrived with a truck at our front door. He told my wife that he owned a heating and air-conditioning company, and for an annual fee (which sounded reasonable) he would provide routine maintenance checks for our systems twice per year in order to prevent anything from going wrong. As he seemed honest and respectable my wife agreed and gave him a check. He said that since he was already there he may as well do his first inspection right away.

He went down into the basement and examined the heating system very carefully. When he was finished he said to my wife "Do you have young children here?"

She said "Yes, we have four."

"What a shame!" he uttered. "It is so dangerous! You are living on the edge of a volcano! This system is about to explode any day now. It is lucky that I came just in time. I will have to put in a new one right away!"

"I will first have to discuss it with my husband when he comes home tonight" answered my wife.

When I came home that night and my wife explained to me what the man had said, I told her that we should ask Jack to come over and give us his opinion before we make any drastic and expensive changes. This we did, and when Jack arrived the next day he examined our system meticulously, and ended off with "Your system is in excellent shape. This man is a thief. Get your money back and get rid of him immediately! If you don't, I will."

On another occasion my wife was called by a financial person who asked her if she was interested in investing in futures. He explained that this was his area of expertise. He assured her that in his hands it was not possible to lose any money as he combined all his investors' money and he invested in many futures wisely. None of his clients, he said, ever lost anything; one could only gain, probably by doubling or trebling one's initial outlay within about three to six months. Being wary, she declined. He kept on calling her about once per month, until after many months she asked me for ten thousand dollars to invest with this man. By now she was convinced that there was no way that she could lose any money. Reluctantly I handed over a check for the said amount.

The following month she called this financial person to enquire how her investment was doing. He told her that she was down about a thousand, but a small loss at the beginning was something that occasionally occurred; however, she should not worry as her investment was sound and would soon be raking in large amounts of money. A month later she called him up again, and she was told that the value had gone down to eight thousand dollars. He reiterated that her investment would soon recover, and she could rest assured that all would be well. This was repeated in the next few months until the value was down to six thousand dollars. I told her to ask for her money back, which she did. She was told that the money could not be withdrawn as it was a small portion of a large pool owned by many individuals. He added that her fears were groundless, and there was no way that she would not be successful in the very near future. He assured her that she was indeed fortunate to be a part of it.

Of course, I ran to Jack for advice. He listened very carefully and without any hesitation said "Get the money out immediately!" I said it was not possible as the gentleman in question had said that the money could not be removed as it was part of a larger investment.

"Give me his number" he stated emphatically. My wife supplied the investment agent's name and number.

The next morning Jack called him and asked for the return of the money. He was given the same answer.

"If I do not receive a check of six thousand dollars from you by Wednesday at noon I will come to your office myself with a police officer and forcibly receive it! In the meantime I have drawn up and sent you legal papers demanding the money." Jack was a lawyer.

By Wednesday noon there was a check for six thousand dollars in Jack's office.

His wife was a beautiful woman and a singer who occasionally performed at jazz clubs and at dances. On one occasion she told him that she had been invited to sing at a Toronto hotel, and she would be away for about two weeks. He said that she should go, and he would be fine at home by himself. When the week-end arrived and he had nothing much to do with himself he decided to pay her a surprise visit. He flew up to Toronto to spend the week-end with her and to listen to her sing. When he arrived there unbeknownst to her he went up to her room, and to his dismay she was in the arms of a fellow musician. That was the end of their marriage.

Then the tragedy occurred. His mother came to visit him in one of his buildings where he had an office on the tenth floor. At the end of her visit she said good-bye and went out into the corridor to get the elevator. She pressed the button to summon the elevator, the door opened and she entered, but there was no elevator, and she tumbled down ten floors. She was dead at the bottom of the elevator shaft in the basement when help arrived. Jack, to say the least, was heart-broken and never discussed the matter again. This had been one of the elevators that Jack had repaired!

During our luncheon Jack informed me, mostly through interpretation by one of his nurses (as it was difficult to understand him) that he handed over all his real estate holdings to his older son who apparently sold some of his buildings for one hundred million dollars. His son was a pilot and had his own private airline which was used to fly executives around the world on business. Passengers could receive haircuts, massage treatment, gourmet meals and entertainment, as well as most other demands that they might order prior to the flight. This was 21st century service for those who could afford it. No other air-line, private or commercial, offers such a variety of services. The son is continuing in the footsteps of his father.

A few days after my meeting with Jack and his entourage they were gone, lost in a different world. I never heard from him again. His life had been embroiled in the crowds and the shuffle of New York City where living was like war, constantly battling and competing in order to win or, at least, to stay alive. He did find time to be of service to others and to give of himself, too. This was important to keep himself sane. The battle of survival is now over, and perhaps now he can find some peace for himself. He is just one more person in the vast panoply of actors that make up the characters of the city of New York.

Simon

I will now introduce you to my friend, Simon. He never knew his mother. She became insane a few weeks after he was born. He was the firstborn – the only one born to her. She had her precious child clinging hungrily to her breast for only a few days. Then her grip grew weaker, and her interest seemed to flag. She did not enjoy anything anymore. Everything became a 'drag' to her. She did not want to eat or talk. She did not wish to speak to her husband when he came home from work. Not even his adoring love for her could melt her heart. She wanted to be alone and to sleep. She was suffering from depression which so frequently follows childbirth, but her case was worse than most. At first the only light in the dark tunnel of her life was this gift that she had received, her wonderful baby with the beautiful dark eyes and soft smiling lips and perfectly formed little body. Soon however, even he could not bring delight to her sad eyes even though she had awaited his arrival so anxiously for so long. Whether he was with her or whether they had taken him away to sleep she remained morose and melancholic. She saw him through a fog, unclearly, blurred as though he was not there, a mirage.

On a sunny morning, looking through her bedroom window she watched her nurse place her newborn child in his baby carriage on a shaded area of the verandah in front of the house. The child was asleep. She saw a cat, or some other animal of that size, jump into the carriage and attack her baby. It must have thought that this was a 'piece of meat' or some other delectable creature. The mother, viewing this horrible scene through the window, emitted a blood-curdling howl and dashed out on to the verandah. She succeeded in chasing the animal away, but when she saw the blood and deep scratches on her baby's face and eyes the heavy cloud in which she was enveloped became even denser and never left her until she died many years later. Clarity of mind never returned. They said she had schizophrenia brought on by childbirth and aggravated by shock.

The nurse called the father who came rushing home from work. He found his wife lying on the cold concrete verandah floor and his baby crying while in his nurse's arms. His blood-soaked face was torn to shreds and his dark eye-balls were oozing blood. The father was unable to interpret what his eyes were seeing. Nor was he able to comprehend the nonsensical words that were gushing forth from his wife's mouth. Only later, with the nurse's interpretation was he able to put the picture together and understand that a creature had violated the privacy of the carriage and might have eaten up his baby if not for his wife's intervention.

The doctor at the hospital told him that the child's wounds would heal and the scars would fade with time, but he was worried about the eye which had been badly damaged. In the fullness of time, however, the eye healed and the vision was unaffected even though there was an obviously large distorted pupil instantly noticeable on seeing him. The only memory he had of his mother was his large black misshapen pupil.

This was the introduction of Simon into the world. He was brought up as a motherless child. His father, who loved him dearly, was unable to take care of him. He had no life's savings and had to earn a living. Simon was farmed out for periods to various aunts and family members for months at a time, and his father came to visit him wherever he was and whenever he could. When he reached school-going age he was sent to boarding school. Vacations were a problem, but his father sent him back to aunts where life was rather boring as there was not too much for a young person to do in the home of an old aunt. He was a quiet lad, rather sad-eyed and always ready to become someone's friend since he had few of his own; he never complained, and did whatever was expected of him.

Simon's father was as good a father as circumstances allowed him to be. Many years later when he met a woman that he wished to marry the law forbade him from doing so as his wife was still alive, even though she had been in a mental institution where she was 'climbing the walls' and eating sand, oblivious to the world around her. In her state of schizophrenia she had no recognition of her husband or son. When Simon was a child his father brought him to visit his mother regularly, but she just stared at them unemotionally and unknowingly, and unaware of whom they were. When she finally moved on from her unknown world to the next she brought some solace to her husband and son. She had done her duty by having brought Simon into the world! But at what a price!

Simon was always sad. He was frequently on his own, even though he did not particularly relish lonesomeness. Boarding school made a man of him, offering him, apart from education, friends, sports, games and a temporary home. Here he could either become a loner or be a member of a large group of boys. Probably because of his general sad demeanor he found himself alone more often than not, but he loved sports. Sport participation was a prominent part of this sort of life. Simon drifted towards the rugby field. He played almost every day, and became rather good at what he was doing. As he grew older his muscles strengthened, and with practice his ability on the field improved. His broad muscular frame caused the other players to beware of this strong, hard playing, fast running forward. He was here, there and everywhere. It was not long before Simon was one of the best players in the team and was eagerly sought after by the coaches. He loved playing the game; he was one of the reasons that his school, and later, his college team was usually at the top of the league.

When the time came to choose a career in life he decided to become a doctor. His father, who had felt guilty for not being able to do more for his son was delighted to extend himself beyond his financial means in order to pay for Simon's education. He was proud to think that despite all the trials and tribulations of the past he would one day become the father of a doctor.

When Simon was about to be sent off by his father to Medical School his father had heard of another young man who, too, was going to the same school. He thought it would be a good idea if both young men should get to know each other and accompany each other. Perhaps they might even become friends. I was that man. We made plans to meet at the railway station just before taking the train to our destination at Rhodes University College in the Eastern Cape Province where we were to do our pre-med studies. We managed to find each other at the train station, and thus commenced a friendship that has lasted until now. We entered the train, and spent most of the time talking to each other. The train was full of numerous students all on their way to school. Some of the students were new and some were old. All mixed and got to know each other, singing and drinking and smoking all the way. Simon and I felt comfortable in our own company. It was better to enter into a new world with a friend rather than be alone. Everything and everybody was unknown in this strange new world, and it would take some time getting used to it all.

We would have preferred to have studied in Johannesburg which was our home town, but the troops were returning from North Africa in World War II, and the university was giving preference for admission to the returning soldiers. Thus there were fewer spaces left for local candidates, so many of the local would-be students had to seek colleges elsewhere.

When Simon and I arrived in this unknown world of hostility we were taken aback. We had never been treated with such disrespect before. We were screamed at and shouted at; we were cursed and made to feel as though we were members of a caste constituting the lowest form of animal life. Some of the new students even cried, and almost all wished to take the next train home. At home we had been treated as little princes; and now suddenly we were like vermin, to be trodden on and, if possible, eliminated. The most pleasant seniors when confronting a new student would become roaring lunatics! As unsuspecting young men, who had only recently been respected seniors and leaders at our high schools, we were now treated as dirt. We were called "inks" as in ink blots – a messy mark on a clean white sheet of paper. We were forced to take cold showers even on wintry mornings under the watchful eyes of the despotic seniors, who were secretly referred to as Nazis. We were ordered to perform all the unpleasant duties for the seniors, and we were made fools of. When a senior approached us we would honestly pray that we would survive the encounter. The only hope was that one day we, too, would become seniors and would be able to inflict the same torture upon the younger ones that would follow us.

However, when they recognized the determination of Simon on the rugby field their hearts melted and he was placed on a pedestal as far as his freshman's status was concerned –"leave him alone". Off the rugby field he had a quiet disposition; there was nothing aggressive about him. However, on the field he was like a leopard on the prowl. He proved to them that he was a better man than they were. They called him "Windhond" which was a whippet, peaceful around the kennel but with maniacal speed and maximal agility when chasing rabbits. Scarcely was there a game played when the sports reporters did not single out Simon for his excellent, or sometimes brilliant performance.

We then moved on to Cape Town University for our medical studies. We had thought that our days of being 'inks' were over, but unfortunately we were beginners all over again at a new university so we went through the same again – but not Simon! He was immediately recognized as the 'windhond', and again was afforded the respect awarded only to heroes. The same record that he had at Rhodes University continued at Cape Town. His speed and agility with which he tore into the opponent's territory was admired by all.

Simon and I became good friends. I continued with my activities and he pursued his on the rugby field. Neither of us sought the limelight. When we got together at the end of the day we would spend hours talking and joking with each other, going for walks, discussing our studies and commiserating with each other. Simon had his rugby practices during the week and matches on week-ends while I joined the long distance and cross country running team. However, we did make friends and became popular within an intimate circle. We could be very humorous at times, and we developed quite a funny to and fro conversational routine that kept the others in the group in stitches. In fact, we often received phone calls from women saying that they were having a party and, even though they had not met us, they were inviting us to the party as they had heard of the funny repertoire that we had put together. Thus on most Saturday nights we were out at parties entertaining the guests. We were like two comedians performing an act. We also had the ability to mimic well known politicians. Of course, the entertainment was free and the invitations kept coming.

There were times when Simon became moody. These periods lasted some days, or even weeks, He would not talk to any of us and kept to himself. If we approached him he would not answer us and would walk away. We knew that the best way to handle this was to leave him alone and that, sooner or later, he would return and become his normal self. He was a hypochondriac. Whenever we studied about a new disease he would decide that he had it. He would run off to the doctor, and come back disappointed that he had been wrong. He started to develop aches and pains, and tried to put his newly gained knowledge to use in order to make a self-diagnosis. Too much knowledge is a dangerous thing, but incomplete knowledge might be even more dangerous. So it was with Simon. He made all sorts of diagnoses that were never confirmed by the medical faculty.

He remained the 'windhond' of the rugby team, but amongst the students he became the focus of teasing and joking. He was known as the man with the floating kidney because his X-ray showed one kidney at a slightly lower level than the other, and he had read that a 'dropped' kidney might be the source of chronic pain. "Simon's kidney is floating out of sight" remarked some of his colleagues. Or he would claim that he had gall-stones or a chronic appendicitis or a torn meniscus depending on what medical condition we were studying at that time. Each new disease would be accompanied by pangs of 'pain' and suffering, and consequently the cause for more sarcasm and teasing from the rest of the student body. These episodes would frequently place him in a self-imposed isolation where he would spend days in his room, only silently appearing for meals, lectures and clinics. However when he emerged from his private quarters from a period that seemed like forever we were all delighted to see him coming out with a smile of embarrassment and readiness to resume the friendship. When he was not under these isolation spells he was liked by all, and he was everybody's friend as he was sensitive, kind and understanding of other people's problems. Throughout these periods of isolation and depression he continued to play his rugby, and his game never seemed to be affected by his internal moods.

So the years went by and our class graduated as medical doctors. Fond farewells were bade as all the newly graduated men and women departed to different parts of the country, most of whom were never to see each other again. They went off to work at different internships, residencies and specialties. Some left the country and went to the United States, England, Israel and Australia. Just as they had been an integrated unit for the past six years, now the unit was shattered and could never be made whole again. Simon went off to work in Pretoria and I returned to my hometown, Johannesburg. We had forged a friendship which was very special. At Medical School everyone knew that we were inseparable friends. Over sixty years have elapsed, but in all that time we have seen each other once or twice. Years would go by without phone calls or letters. One might have surmised that there must have been a falling out in the relationship, but it was not the case. Every now and then there would be a contact by phone, and it would seem as though time had not passed by. It would be like the old days. We had each gone in different directions and followed our own stars. Simon ended up in Australia and I wound up in the United States. He and his wife came to see us once while we were living in New York, and it seemed as though we had not been apart for so long. Simon had married Henrietta and they had four children in South Africa, one of whom followed in his father's footsteps and became a doctor. After his children grew up they migrated to Australia. When Simon retired he followed his children there. His grandson also became a doctor. Thus there were now three generations of doctors in the family.

I hear from him occasionally from Australia and I receive a photograph now and then, but we don't expect to be together ever again. We are left with memories of happiness and sadness, punctuated by laughter. Memories invoke feelings of nostalgia; and what can be sweeter than that?

Sylvia

Then there was Sylvia, as pretty and as bright as her name suggests. She was born in Manhattan and went to school there. She had numerous friends and was very popular with both men and women. She went to college, but never finished her studies because she was caught up in a love affair with another student. Instead of graduating she married and became pregnant with a beautiful daughter, Cindy, to whom she devoted most of her time as she did not have a job. Her husband was at work all day, and she spent most of her time taking care of the home and bringing up her daughter.

Her new-found motherhood robbed her of her husband as all her love was showered upon her daughter. Her days of bliss and contentment enabled him to fall in love with his secretary. Sylvia and her husband soon divorced, leaving her as a single parent. This cruel blow that came out of the blue was partially of her own making. It shattered her faith in men as she realized that what she thought was true love had turned out to be a chimera. Fortunately the divorce settlement took care of any possible financial problems with which she might have been faced.

Sylvia was unprepared for her new life of being a single parent to a child who had been brought up with all the love and comforts and toys that she desired. Now the future seemed dark and inhospitable. It appeared as though nothing was secure, and happiness was only temporary. Sylvia became a nervous wreck.

She became neurotic. She was unprepared for a life without her husband who had been a great support for her as long as the romance lasted. She was afraid to drive a car because, if she got killed, who would take care of Cindy? Nor did she wish to fly again. What would happen if there was a problem and the plane lost its power in mid-air? She was afraid to cross the road even when the traffic signals gave pedestrians the right to walk. What if a crazy person who did not observe the road signs drove through and killed her? She had panic attacks when at times she did not even trust herself with Cindy. She sought the services of a psychotherapist, but it was difficult to break through her deep fears.

Sylvia was saved by Prince Charming in the form of Edgar. Edgar was a textile producer of expensive men's suits. He was a wealthy man who had recently divorced. Even though his divorce had cost him a great deal of money it was only a bucketful in the sea of his assets. He was both enamored of and sympathetic towards Sylvia and her fears. It did not take very long for him to decide that being married to Sylvia and becoming a parent to young Cindy was what he most desired. Edgar and Sylvia were soon united and he adopted Cindy as his own daughter. He and Sylvia went out dancing and dining – life became one glorious holiday. They took exotic vacations to far-flung islands on distant oceans. They explored cities and beaches and jungles all over the world. They were a happy closely knit family. Her neurosis never really left her. She was still afraid to cross the road alone or drive a car.

One day when Sylvia felt a lump in her breast she was afraid to mention it to anybody, even her close friends. She certainly was not telling Edgar or Cindy – and visiting a doctor would only invite further investigation, which would take away all the fun they were having together as a family. No, she would keep this a secret, and maybe the lump would disappear.

Somehow, she finally spilt the news to Edgar rather nonchalantly one day. He immediately made an appointment with a surgeon whom she was reluctant to visit. Nevertheless, he accompanied her on her appointment. Tests, X-rays, ultra-sounds and biopsies followed. The breast harbored a cancerous tumor. It was removed, as were the surrounding lymph-nodes including those in the arm-pit. Alas, the cancer had spread well beyond the confines of the breast rendering all the surrounding lymph-nodes cancerous. Radiation and chemotherapy were ordered, but Sylvia said "No, this is where I draw the line". She refused to accept either. "You will be dead in six months if you have no further treatment" warned her doctors. "Your cancer has penetrated all the lymph-nodes in your arm-pits, which constitute the outer defenses of your breast" they said. Edgar and Cindy pleaded with her to accept the doctor's orders, as did all her friends.

She refused to budge. She said "This is my body. I will not take any more treatment". There was nothing more anybody could do about it.

And so it was. This frightened, panic-stricken woman who would not cross the road by herself had now made a heroic decision (perhaps unwise, in the light of medical knowledge) to be responsible for her own life as long as she was alive. Whereas she had lived a frightened timorous life until she received a severe threat to her existence, she now decided to live according to her dictates. She started reading books by cancer survivors, she did exercises, she eliminated meat from her diet, she swallowed different herbs and sea-weed from the Orient and she ate certain foods that she had read about in her books. She took control of her own treatment. No longer was she going to take orders from others. She would from now on make her own decisions. She would not visit any more doctors.

Despite a serious prognosis hanging over her head she decided not to waste any more time and to continue her education which had been aborted at the time of her first marriage. She received her B.A. and M.A. degrees, and then she went on to graduate with a doctorate in psychology. Gradually she overcame her fears and obsessions due to the strength she was developing within her own mind. All this time she never went to see a doctor for a medical check-up for her condition or consult anyone about herself. She went about her life, enjoying herself and taking care of husband and child. She opened up a practice for administering psychotherapy to the consternation of her husband and daughter. Her practice grew and her fame spread by word of mouth, and soon she was running a busy practice and controlling a fairly large staff.

She pushed all thoughts of her medical diagnosis into the background and lived a full life with her family. Her practice kept growing. Those who knew her in her earlier days when she was nervous and timorous could only gasp in awe when they saw this unrecognizable woman in action.

She lived like this for seventeen years, a different woman with a different life. She never complained and never felt sorry for herself. She and her husband went to Florida for a vacation, and they came to visit us. We all went for a walk along the beach one evening, and I was walking with her. She told me that she had noticed tumor re-growth in her arm-pit and on her chest wall, but she had not informed her husband and daughter about this. I told her to go and see a doctor about this. She said that it was too late now, but she had gained seventeen years of a wonderful life without treatment. She expected to die soon. Had she accepted radiation and chemotherapy she was sure that she would have been dead a long time ago.

However, they went home the next day. On the Sunday afternoon after their return, she said to Edgar "It is a lovely day today. Why don't you and Cindy take a walk in Central Park?" They lived opposite Central Park in Manhattan.

"Come with us" they invited her.

"No, I think that I will take a nap. I'm feeling a little tired".

Off they went, father and daughter. When they returned they found Sylvia asleep. They came back into the room a little later to see if she was still sleeping. On closer inspection they saw that she was dead. By her side was a syringe emptied of its contents.

That was another thread which is a part of the quilt that makes up New York.

Dennis

Let me tell you about Dennis. This goes back to my days in South Africa. I was a doctor on the staff of the hospital which belonged to a large gold mine in a small town. In fact, at that time it was the largest gold mine in the world. Dennis was the magistrate of the town. I met him and we became good friends. He was married and had two daughters. I was still unmarried. Dennis did not receive a large salary in his job. He knew that he would require a larger income in order to buy a home and to educate his two daughters and give his family the life that he knew that they deserved

As the senior medical officer to the hospital I was entitled to the house that was a part of the hospital complex. It was a large home, and I felt guilty occupying it by myself and living like a prince. When Dennis and I discussed this together one day we both hit up on the idea that it might be a good idea if his family moved in and we lived together. They would have the full run of the house. I would have my quarters. His wife would be in charge of the housekeeping, the cooking and the servants. There was no exchange of money, no rent; we each understood our obligations. We would both gain from the situation.

So we tried out the experiment. It had been an excellent idea, as we lived together for about seven years. We each went about our lives in our own ways, often eating together, sometimes entertaining together. The girls had their own friends. Dennis went to court every day, Madge (his wife) was a school teacher, and I worked at the hospital. Dennis was saving quite a lot of money. After another year Dennis gave up his job as a magistrate, and started work in a legal office in Johannesburg which handled trademarks and copyrights. This gave him a better income and greater prospects for the future. We had large grounds where the girls could play with their friends. There were fruit trees and a vegetable garden. We even had a chicken coop, producing our own eggs. We were one happy family.

Dennis was an Afrikaner. The white population of South Africa consisted mainly of English-speaking and Afrikaans-speaking people. Most Afrikaners were members of the National Party, which was the Party in power. They ran the government from 1948 to 1994. This was the notorious apartheid government, which, while it was in power, was isolated and received the wrath of most of the outside world because of its policies of racial discrimination against the non-white people in the country.

Even though most of Dennis' family and friends supported the National Party, he was not a member nor did he vote for them. You might think that he was not politically inclined. That was not so. Dennis was very aware of what was going on and was a member of the opposition groups, making him an outcast amongst his own people. In fact, he was one of the founders of the Progressive Party which stood for equality amongst all people and accepted Black and Colored members into its ranks. This was the first party in the country that was prepared to bring the Blacks into the government. If this does not sound revolutionary, it certainly was for South Africa. Even the main opposition Party (the United Party) which gave lip service to equality amongst races, never allowed a Black man in as a member. Blacks, of course, had no vote even though they were 80% of the population. Dennis had a great empathy for the Bantu in South Africa. He befriended many, and some came to our house, which was a very dangerous move as the law of the land warned against any socialization with the Blacks and could send one to jail.

I was fortunate to meet and talk to the important figures in this new Progressive Party as many of the meetings were held in our house. Dennis and his Party made the first inroads that helped to fight for the necessity of the Black vote in the country and the introduction of civil rights. The Progressives won a number of seats in the parliamentary elections. This was only the beginning. The opposition to the government by the Progressive Party was far greater than the weak efforts that had hitherto been provided by the United Party in the past.

From this point onwards things began to change. The children of the Boers (the Afrikaner farmers) did not have the same outlook as their fathers. Their forefathers had fought and trekked to make this country theirs, and kept the native population down in order to maintain their personal and political security. Their children were born into security. Instead of becoming farmers like their parents they went to the universities and studied to become professionals. They began to believe in equality among the races and fair play. At the same time the outside world had placed sanctions upon South Africa because of the policy of apartheid. There were boycotts of South African exports and sports teams. These pressures began to bear fruit. There were pleas from the whole world to free Nelson Mandela. Forced into a corner, the South African government complied. Mandela who had been imprisoned for about twenty-five years was freed, the Blacks were given a vote for the first time, and the Whites were driven out of power.

Of course, all this did not happen because of Dennis and the Progressive Party, but he was one in the forefront of a small group in the fight for democracy in South Africa. He was not afraid to speak out despite the general opinions all over the land and, particularly around him. The government was jailing people who supported equal rights for Black people.

The aftermath of the introduction of democracy into South Africa was an overdose of crime – murders, robberies, rapes, house break-ins and muggings. The ever-vigilant police from the apartheid era were gone, and the new breath of freedom brought on an incentive to commit crime. For some it might have been a desire for revenge. There was almost a state of anarchy in many areas.

Nobody ever attempted to break-in or rob Dennis' home. All the Black people knew that he had been a friend to them during the dark days. Most people locked their homes, had attack dogs to guard their homes and some even had electrified fences for their protection, but Dennis left his front door unlocked, and nobody dared to enter his home illegally. Wherever he went he was treated with respect, even after he retired from politics. Those who knew the muggers and the robbers warned them that they would be reported to the police if they did anything to harm Dennis or his family.

He was a kind and simple person; he saw good in all people. Everybody was his friend. People would come in all day and most of the night to see Dennis and Madge or ask for advice. Many slept over. When a young girl in the town lost her father while her mother was being treated in a drug addiction center for drug over-use and alcoholism, he invited her to stay at his home. When the alcoholic mother deteriorated too far to be of any value to this girl and herself Dennis adopted the young girl. She lived with Dennis' family and became a nurse, reaching the highest ranks in her profession at the Johannesburg hospital. Thanks to Dennis' interference he not only saved her life but he also made her a most respected medical professional. She was not the only young person that Dennis helped. There were other young people that he assisted morally and financially, encouraging them to give of their most and aiding them with their educational fees.

He was always doing things to help people. He was a member of the international Lions Club, which was a group of people dedicated to helping humanity throughout the world. He reached the status of being the president of the Lions Club for Africa and South-East Asia.

During World War II he had been in the Royal Air Force. No, he was not a pilot, but his job was to monitor all planes that flew out on bombing missions and he had to make sure that each plane returned. Raids took place during all hours of the day and night, and so he remained awake most of the day and night to do his audit. Consequently he seldom had a full night's sleep, relying on cat naps. When the war was over, he told me that he continued with the same pattern of short naps since he had become so inured with this habit. He never had a full night's sleep, resting only with cat naps.

I felt a part of his family. It was a bitter sweet day when I had to approach them and tell them that I was going to get married, and that there would have to be a parting of our ways. We did so graciously, knowing that our friendship had been invaluable to all of us. The years we spent together enabled him to save some money and placed him in a better financial situation. We remained special friends after that until both Dennis and Madge passed away. Their two daughters are happily married and mothers of grown-up children. They still call me Uncle Doctor.

Dennis was a rare individual. He knew what was right, and fought for it. He was selfless; he only wished to help others, not superficially – but until there were positive results. While he was a magistrate he once sentenced a Black man to a term of hard labor. This man had received multiple such sentences in the past. When his sentence was over, Dennis feared for this man's future as he saw that his life was going nowhere, so he offered him a job in our garden in order to give him an opportunity to improve his life and also so that he, Dennis, could watch over him. He worked for us for many years, and performed well without any arrests or drunken spells added to his record.

There was not a drop of racism in Dennis' blood. I know that he loved all people, and he seemed to instill that characteristic among those with whom he was in contact. He certainly affected me. He was a world citizen who loved his fellow man. He could dine with kings as well as lowly peons. His true politics was to give a helping hand to anyone who could use it and would benefit from it. I look upon him as a brother. I think of him very often even though he lives no longer, and I miss him. I know that he affected my life more than I have realized.

Seymour

Now allow me to tell you of someone else. There are some people who appear to be not from this world. Nor are they from Mars since they are not war-like, but they are different. They do not seem to have the same values as the rest of us. They are not competitive, and do not strive for greater riches or power or fame. They seek beauty in art, in music, in the universe. They want to see things right, balanced, correct. When they are comfortable with the state of their art or music they are happy with their lives. If not, they are not in sync with life and cannot find peace. This is their Nirvana. Such a man is Seymour.

Seymour was a pianist, and a very successful one at that. He started playing the piano as a child, and by the age of fifteen he was already giving piano lessons. He became a concert pianist, travelling the world circuits in the large concert halls in the US and Europe, receiving rave reviews wherever he went. But that was not what he wanted. He was not really interested in showing how great he was as a pianist; he did not like the pangs of nervousness that beset him (and all other artistes before a performance) and he scarcely enjoyed the travelling and hotel stays that inevitably accompanied this type of work. So he retired from the concert circuit early in life, and decided to do what he wanted to do – and that was to teach. He would teach others to play the piano in the method in which pianos ought to be played. No more travelling, no more stage-fright! Now he could be himself and do what he always wanted to do. He loved the discipline, the rhythm and the emotion of music.

It was during this period of his life that I came upon Seymour. My son, Darron, was receiving piano lessons from a family friend who, too, had been a concert pianist. After many months of lessons his piano teacher approached my wife and I, and admitted to us that she was unable to make much progress with Darron; but she had an idea that there was one man who, she knew, could. You see, Darron has a good ear for music and is gifted with a talent for it but is a subject of Asperger's Syndrome and suffers from an obsessional-compulsive disorder. The man who could help Darron, she said, was her own teacher, Seymour. She warned us that Seymour only took on students who were advanced and excellent players but anyhow "Why don't you tell Seymour that I referred you to him, and see what he thinks?"

So she made an appointment for us, and off to Seymour we went. We arrived at his one-room studio apartment in Manhattan, and he spent an hour listening to Darron play while my wife and I went walking around the neighborhood. When we returned Seymour said to us "He has a wonderful ear for music. There is something about him that makes him a challenge for me to teach him. I normally only teach advanced students or people who are preparing for a concert at Alice Tully Hall or Carnegie Hall, but I am looking forward to having Darron as a student".

Through Seymour's guidance Darron became an accomplished pianist despite his psychological drawbacks. For many years he continued as Seymour's student, and even after we re-located to Florida Darron flew to New York every two weeks to take two lessons with Seymour.

Seymour became a friend of the family. We met, and became friendly with many of his students. It was like a large happy family. They often came to our house and played the piano for us. We attended their concerts and master classes. Darron, too, performed at some smaller recitals. Seymour was in his element with his team of followers. Being Seymour's student became a way of life. Through the art of music he was able to display much wisdom about life in general. I cannot imagine anyone else to be more dedicated to music than he is. He was not interested in the dramatic presentation of music as some egocentric exponents might infuse themselves into the work where the listener becomes more aware of the artiste than the opus. He was interested in presenting a true interpretation of the piece without forcing his presence into the scene. All these years Seymour was also composing music, and he has published many volumes of music as well as books, such as "With My Own Two Hands" in order to help the student in his understanding.

He wanted nothing luxurious or ostentatious for himself. He lived – and still lives - in the same studio apartment for over fifty years. His home is there so that he can be involved with music. He is comfortable in his own skin. At night his living room becomes his bedroom after a sofa is turned into a bed and a few sticks of furniture are moved around. By day, everything reverts in order to become a living room-studio. His kitchen is one counter-top and a toaster oven. He never owned a car; he either walked or used public transportation, and continues to do so. He never married, although there were women in his life. He did not want the responsibility of a wife and children as this would detract from his true love which was music. Nobody could possibly imagine the depth of the soul and the breadth of the intellect of this quiet, modest, simple and kind person until they get to know him.

Fortunately Seymour's life has not gone unnoticed. Recently Ethan Hawke, a noted actor and producer, was sitting next to Seymour at a dinner party. He realized that this was no ordinary man who was eating beside him. He spent a great deal of time talking to him and got to know him better. He asked Seymour if he could visit him at his home and sit in on some of his lessons. Seymour said that he could do so. He came many times and spoke to his students, thereby getting to know Seymour and his past life much better. He spoke to many music experts about Seymour. The result is a movie called "Seymour – A Life".

To Seymour music is a way of life, and everything else must take a back seat. Music is a language, an art, a technique and a way of expressing one's emotions. In short, music is life itself. To Seymour life without music would be pointless. Music is not a part of his life. It is his life. The world exists so that there should be music.

CHAPTER 4

Moses

Did he exist or didn't he? Was he one person or was he a composite of a number of people? Was he a Jew or was he an Egyptian? It all happened so long ago at a time when historical events were not properly recorded by the Hebrews, but were only written millennia later. We are influenced by information from different sources written long after the events took place, and we need to separate possible truth from probable exaggeration, lies and propaganda, but we will probably never know the real truth. In the days of the pharaohs Egypt was an advanced country, and they did record history, documenting events in detail in hieroglyphics; yet there is no mention of the Jews as slaves. There is no archaeological evidence of a Jewish presence in Egypt at that time, even though they were there for four hundred years. There are no specimens or shards of pottery left behind by a people who wondered through the Sinai desert for forty years. Famous historians, such as Josephus and Philo, wrote about Moses, but from where did they get their information as he was supposed to have lived almost two thousand years before them? Yet we do know that Moses is revered by Judaism, Christianity and Islam. He is considered as a Prophet and a human being born of human parents, unlike Jesus who was the son of God. He was the person to whom God entrusted major undertakings and responsibilities. He is one of the most important characters in the history of the Jews. 'Moshe Rabenu' is how he is known – 'Moses, Our Teacher'. Unlike most of us he spoke to God often and, on occasion, even disagreed with Him, so we are told. He was the one who had to speak to his people for God and to God for his people. He sometimes had to kill for Him!

It all started with Joseph. Joseph, son of Jacob and Rachel, was the first Israelite to arrive in Egypt, according to the Old Testament. He arrived as a slave because he was sold by his envious and feuding brothers to a group of travelers going to Egypt. Years later his eleven brothers and their father also came to Egypt with a group of their countrymen because there was a famine in the land of their forefathers. They came in order to survive. This was the beginning of the Israelite presence in Egypt.

Joseph rose in importance, graduating from slave to high office in the land of his adoption until he became adviser to Pharaoh, but his brothers and their friends soon became slaves unto Pharaoh, and remained as such. This group of Israelites living in the land of their adoption multiplied and lived as a community in Goshen. They performed the heavy labor for their Egyptian taskmasters and built the cities of Ramses and Pithom. It is said that they built the pyramids, but that was impossible as the pyramids were there long before they were supposed to have arrived. After about four or five hundred years their population had vastly grown. Pharaoh feared that one day the slaves may revolt and cause him trouble – they may even take over the country! He decreed that every male Israelite child must be put to death at birth so as to curb their population growth. When the midwives did not perform their jobs as prescribed by Pharaoh, Puah, the lead midwife, explained that the Israelite women were so strong that they delivered their own babies before the midwives arrived! Pharaoh then decided the only way to go was death by drowning.

Under these circumstances a baby boy was born to Amram and Yochevet. The mother, Yochevet, did not wish to give up her child Moses according to Pharaoh's decree so she hid him for three months. When she could hide him no longer, it is said, she placed him in a basket made from bulrushes, and water-proofed it with bitumen and tar. She then took the young boy in the basket and allowed it to float down the River Nile.

Pharaoh's daughter found him in his basket. Coincidentally, Miriam who was Moses' sister happened to be present at that time on the banks of the river. She asked Pharaoh's daughter if she required a nurse to help her raise the baby, whereupon she said yes. Miriam went home to get her mother and brought her to the palace. Thus Yochevet was present at her child's upbringing and during his impressionable years. He was brought up in the palace in the midst of luxury and, we presume, with a fine education, the best that Egypt could offer. Moshe was his Hebrew name; it means 'to draw', which was what Pharaoh's daughter did – she drew him out of the water. It is also an Egyptian name, meaning 'son of', as in Pharaoh Thutmose or Ramses. Unfortunately this does not help us decide his origin, Jewish or Egyptian.

Moses turned out to be a leader of his people. Apparently leaders of people are sometimes drawn out of water. Sargon the Great, King of Akkadia, who was the illegitimate son of a priestess, born about a thousand years before Moses, too, was placed in a basket protected with bitumen and tar, and left floating down the Euphrates River by his mother. He was plucked out of the water and raised by a gardener. Sargon also became a great leader of his people. This was all recorded at the time in the cuneiform writings. Is the story of Moses' beginnings true or is this a copy of the Sargon story? Are we sure that Moses, the deliverer of his people, is the same person as the child who was placed in the River Nile? Distinguishing fact from fiction is often blurred and we are frequently misled by the text.

When Moses was a young man he saw a Hebrew being attacked by an Egyptian, whereupon he approached the Egyptian and killed him, and buried him in the desert sand. Did he protect the man because he felt akin to him as a Hebrew or would he, as a moral and just person, have protected any man who was brutally and unfairly attacked? The news of the murder leaked out, apparently through another Hebrew who witnessed the slaying. Moses ran away in order to escape discovery and certain death. He crossed the Sinai Peninsula, and arrived in Midian, according to the Bible.

Josephus, a Jewish historian who became a Roman citizen, lived at the time of Jesus. He said that when Moses ran away from Egypt he first went to Ethiopia, where he was praised and respected for his power and great physique. He fought on the side of the Ethiopian king, married an Ethiopian woman with whom he had no children, and became a general in their army. He had lived in Ethiopia until he was about forty years old. He was about to be made king of Ethiopia after the passing of the ruler at that time, but when opposition to his appointment arose on account of his alien origin, he left his wife and only then fled and ran away to Midian. His siblings Miriam and Aaron scolded him later while they were crossing the Sinai Desert, for having married an Ethiopian.

One day, after arriving in Midian, he saw a Midianite harassing a group of women at a well, and noticed that he was preventing them from getting drinking water for their sheep. Moses helped the girls, who were sisters, overcome the man's bullying, and made sure that their livestock received the drinking water that they required. When the sisters returned home they told their father about the kind stranger who had assisted them at the well. The father asked them to bring this man home to meet him. This they did. The father's name was Jethro, also known as Hobab. Apparently Moses and Jethro struck up a friendship, and Moses married one of his daughters, Zipporah. He remained in Midian for forty years, and had two sons with Zipporah - Gershon and Eliezer. While living in Midian he served as a shepherd to Jethro, often taking his cattle into the Sinai Peninsula to graze.

Or maybe he did not strike up a friendship with Jethro. According to Josephus, (we do not know his source of information) Moses was held as a prisoner in a dungeon by Jethro for many years, and was fed only bread and water. Apparently Zipporah came every day and stealthily supplied him with extra food and added comforts. Only after Jethro freed him did he marry Zipporah and take care of Jethro's livestock.

Jethro was a wise man. He is considered to be from the family of the offspring of Abraham, which places him in holy territory. Even though he was not an Israelite he was a teacher of Moses, giving him much sound advice. The concept of Yahweh came from Jethro, as did many other customs which were taken over from the Midianites by the Jews via Moses. The Druzes of Northern Israel, Lebanon, Jordan and Syria follow the teachings of Jethro. They visit his tomb in Tiberias whenever they get the opportunity to do so. They are not Muslims, even though they share certain beliefs with them, nor are they Christians despite the fact that they follow some Christian teachings. Most of the Druze living in Israel have a loyalty to the Jewish state. They serve in the Israeli army and in the Knesseth; yet the Syrian Druze are loyal to Syria. By checking on their DNA it has been found that many Druze are of Jewish descent.

Moses must have felt an outcast for the many years since he ran away from Egypt in order to preserve his life. He also ran away from Ethiopia, and now he was a lonely shepherd for his father-in-law. His first son was named Gershon, which means 'banished' or 'alien', a rather sad name, perhaps expressing his mood at that time. Things seemed to have improved when his second son was born – Eliezer, meaning 'God is my help', a little more inspiring name.

Moses saw God for the first time when he was out with Jethro's livestock; he witnessed the Burning Bush, which was supposed to have been at the site of Mount Sinai where he later received the Ten Commandments. Noticing that it burned but did not consume itself he looked deeper and saw God in the bush. When he questioned the Bush as to who He was he received the answer "I am what I am". God told him to go back to Egypt and save the Israelite slaves by bringing them out of Egypt and leading them to the Holy Land. He warned him that it would not be easy as Pharaoh would not wish to let them go. However, God had a plan that would finally overcome Pharaoh's desire to hold on to his slaves.

Moses and his family now return to the Holy Land in order to carry out God's will. Once having instructed him to take his people out of bondage God does an about-face! The Book of Exodus says that God wanted to kill Moses. Why should He want to do that after having chosen him among all others for the huge task of saving his People? One day He appoints a General, and the next day He wants him killed! Because Moses was not circumcised! God had made a covenant with His people through Abraham that all males must be circumcised, and here was the newly installed leader uncircumcised! After he was born circumcision was not a reality because he was hidden by his mother for fear of losing her child since all Israelite boys were to be killed by the Egyptian authorities soon after birth. Having been brought up in Pharaoh's palace he never had the opportunity to get circumcised. As a grown man he probably never thought of it or did not want to be involved in a painful and dangerous procedure. He never lived in Goshen amongst the Jews so there was no pressure to be circumcised. Certainly during the years that he was in Ethiopia and Midian there was no possibility of having it done. Excuses have been made by some apologists that he had a small foreskin. This should make no difference as the covenant calls for circumcision of all Hebrew males, and does not specify on the type of foreskin. Some rabbis have said that Moses was born circumcised. God's instructions to Abraham (Gen. 17) were that any male who was not circumcised would be cut off from his people. It does not talk of exempting those who appear to have been born circumcised or to have had a small foreskin. This is obviously a cop-out. Everybody has some foreskin. If God knew that he had a small or absent foreskin and therefore had not been circumcised why should he want to kill him?

Abraham circumcised himself at the age of 99. The Zohar says that any man who is not circumcised cannot commune with God, yet no man has communed with God more than the uncircumcised Moses did. During forty years in the desert there were no circumcisions performed by the Israelites. However, just before they entered the Promised Land Joshua circumcised all males.

Nevertheless, Moses was saved by Zipporah, a non-Jew, a Midianite woman, when she became aware of God's intentions (Ex. 4:24-26). She circumcised her son, Gershon – a less difficult job - and placed his foreskin between Moses' feet. The Bible uses the word 'feet' when it means genitalia. Apparently the Book is self-censored. Even though it was not Moses, but his son who had been circumcised by Zipporah's action, Moses' life was saved, and he was permitted to continue with his leadership role. Was the good Lord really fooled, thinking that the foreskin sitting between Moses' feet had belonged to him? Could it be that the Creator of the universe who is aware of everything from the precision of the timing of the planetary orbits as well as the thoughts going on in people's minds, was tricked by Zipporah's ruse? After this,

Zipporah went back to Midian with her two sons. We hear very little of them again.

Moses' life was saved by four women on different occasions. His mother had prevented him from being killed after birth by the authorities when all Jewish males were to be put to death. Then Pharaoh's daughter drew him out of the water and brought him to the palace instead of giving him up. His sister, Miriam, made sure that his mother would nurse him in the palace and keep an eye on him. And now, Zipporah saves his life again! Imagine that – a non-Israelite woman circumcising her son! Apparently this move satisfied the Lord, as he allowed Moses to get on with the task of delivering the Israelite slaves out of Egypt. Is it not strange to contemplate that the greatest all-time hero of the Jews and the man who spoke to God more than anyone else was never circumcised – and therefore not a Jew? As the Bible states, he should have been cut off from his people!

As Moses was a stutterer, God told him to take his brother Aaron with him in order to speak to Pharaoh. When Moses and Aaron told Pharaoh that God had sent them he was unaware of who this God was. The Egyptians had many gods, but they had never heard of this one, an all-encompassing God without any particular specialty, like a general practitioner – unlike any that Pharaoh had ever known. In Egypt each god practiced in his own field of expertise.

The Book of Exodus describes the Ten Plagues that were inflicted upon the Egyptians in order to get Pharaoh to permit the Jews to leave. The Plagues consisted of a series of calamities which were meant to harm the Egyptians in such a way that Pharaoh would allow the Israelites to leave. The Israelites were untouched by these plagues. After each plague Moses was told that his people could go, but then "God hardened Pharaoh's heart" and he changed his mind. First, water was turned into blood (only for the Egyptians); then came the frogs jumping all over the land. This was followed by lice, and later, flies. Disease of the livestock probably was the result of the flies. The next plague brought boils to the Egyptian people. Hail then fell upon the land destroying all in its wake, and the greenery that survived was eaten up by locusts, and then followed darkness. Darkness was a response to show the Egyptians that

Yahweh was more powerful than the Egyptian god of light. The final plague – the slaying of the firstborn - was too much for the suffering Egyptians to tolerate. Whereupon, Pharaoh finally allowed Moses' to let his people go!

Archaeological studies have determined that there were many calamities that beset the Egyptians during a period of their history, but they place the timing to be many centuries before Moses. The exodus probably occurred about 1448 B.C. Are Moses and the Israelites the benefactors of the story of Sargon and the Ten Plagues and the construction of the Pyramids, all three of which seem to have preceded them? The Plagues are not really miracles as suggested in the Bible. They can be explained as naturally occurring phenomena – even the water turning to blood could be caused by certain algae that turn the water red. Insects, vermin and frogs are infestations that frequently fall upon inhabitants on this planet. The fact that all these calamities struck the Egyptians, and not the Hebrews, might be because the Hebrews were living in a different area – in Goshen. The slaying of the first-born might be a little more difficult to explain – perhaps an infectious disease epidemic like meningococcal meningitis struck a particular region in which the Hebrews were not residing.

So it was the enemy of the Jews (the Egyptians) who supplied the Jews with their leader. Either he was brought up in their palace where he received education and training, according to Exodus, or he was an Egyptian, according to Freud. Without any proof available, can we believe that the little boy who was placed in the river by his mother was the same person that was plucked out of the Nile by Pharaoh's daughter and delivered the Jews eighty years later? Moses was eighty years old when he started his exodus through the Sinai Desert. He was forty years old when he arrived in Midian and lived there for forty years. There are those who believe that Moses was an Egyptian who belonged to a group who had monotheistic beliefs.

Whether Moses was a Jew or not he certainly spent no time living with Jews or carrying out any of their religious rites or customs. From where could he have learnt them? He was put into a basket in the river when he was three months old. He was brought up in Pharoah's palace and lived there until he was a young man. Then he ran away to Ethiopia and Midian, and lived most of his adult life there. He only arrived in Goshen to lead the Jews back to the Holy Land when he was eighty. Therefore he never lived with Jews and really knew very little about them. He was a stranger amongst his own people. Why should they have trusted him?

There was a Pharaoh Akhenaten who believed in only one God, and even though this was not a popular belief in Egypt at that time he had some followers. Most Egyptians believed in and wanted many gods. Freud suggested that the monotheism of Akhenaten might have influenced Moses to lead a number of fellow believers out of the country so as to gain freedom from slavery, and also so that they could practice their own beliefs freely. Some have even written that Moses and Akhenaten are one and the same person.

There were supposed to have been 600,000 adult Israelite males and their families that left Egypt. This could mean about a million or more people. Remember less than 100 arrived with Joseph's brothers about four to five hundred years before that. Soon after they departed in a hurry Pharaoh changed his mind and decided to send his charioteers to chase them and bring them back. The so-called miracle of the Israelites crossing the Red Sea on dry land and the drowning of the Egyptian charioteers in the Red Sea can be explained perhaps by an error in the translation. Apparently it was not the Red Sea that was crossed (as described in the English texts of the Bible), but the Reed Sea to the north of the Red Sea. The Hebrew Bible never mentioned the Red Sea; it talks of the Yum Suf, which means the Reed Sea; it is no longer in existence as it has been replaced by the Suez Canal which was built by de Lesseps and French engineers at the end of the nineteenth century. Moses knew this part of the country well, having traversed the territory many times. He ran away after killing a man on his way to Midian and he had also been a shepherd of Jethro's flocks for forty years in Midian, so he was well aware of the marshes and bogs and quicksand and dry areas of the Reed Sea which enabled him to lead the Israelites safely across on dry land. The charioteers did not know this part of Egypt; they were 'city slickers', thus they rushed right into the deep waters and quicksand, knowing that Moses and his people had recently passed through; and they drowned!

Moses was supposed to have been strong, very handsome and tall. He was also wealthy. It is said that his wealth came from Jethro, or did he gain his wealth from the gold that the Israelites took out of Egypt with them? We are told that he had a halo around his face and head which appeared on him after confronting the Lord at the Burning Bush. Apart from speaking to God on numerous occasions it is said that he was able to prophesy the future.

The march across the Sinai Desert should have taken perhaps a month or two but it took forty years. It was a trek full of ups and downs. There were high points and low. The Israelites were unhappy and grumbled saying that they wanted to go home. It would be better, they said, to have died as slaves in Egypt than to spend the rest of their days wandering about the desert. They worshipped idols and built a Golden Calf. They faced hardships and wars. They died of natural causes or were killed by marauding tribesmen. Apparently the trek proved to be a hazardous journey, even though the Lord supplied manna by day and quail by night. The appearance of manna was considered to have been a miracle, but Bedouins in the Sinai Desert see it all the time. It is a result of a reaction of plant lice on the sap from the tamarisk tree creating an edible substance which contains carbohydrates and could have kept them alive for long periods. They were told to eat the manna before the sun rises because when the days get hot the manna melts into the earth.

Even Moses disobeyed God at Meribah when He told him to speak to the rock and tell it to produce water – in which case it would have been treated as a miracle from God when water suddenly appeared. Instead Moses struck the rock with his rod without mentioning to it that it should produce water, and the water gushed out. By striking the rock and not speaking to it in the name of God, it looked as though Moses had brought forth the water himself, taking the credit away from God. God never forgave him for this. In the Ten Commandments God tells us that he is a jealous God.

Striking rocks with wands in the Sinai Desert and producing water is not as miraculous as it might appear to be. During World War I a

British officer crossing the desert in the same area thought that he was about to perish from thirst when his Arab guide cracked a rock in front of him with a hammer, and water gushed forth. There is a superficial subterranean aquifer in many areas of the Sinai Desert.

According to some sources Moses' rod has a history. It is said to have been designed by Adam in the Garden of Eden from the twig of a fig tree; then it was handed down to his sons, landing up in the hands of Enoch, who gave it to his son Noah. Somehow Jacob had it when he arrived in Egypt. It finally ended up in Pharaoh's palace, where we know that Joseph was adviser to the Pharaoh. Jethro, of all people, who later, too, became an adviser to Pharaoh, saw it in the palace grounds and took it. It was Jethro who gave the rod to Moses.

The Israelites in the desert were an unruly mob. True, they suffered many hardships; they were attacked by the Amalekites; they went through days of hunger and thirst and the effects caused by the elements. They were not 'happy campers'; they were nostalgic for their lives in Goshen. They were constantly engaging in idolatry, and even Aaron, the brother of Moses, who should have set a better example, was a culprit helping to build the golden calf. According to the Muslims the Jews were originally God's Chosen People, but when they continued to worship idols and the golden calf the honor was taken away from them, and now the Muslims are the Chosen Race.

Beautiful Midianite women arrived with their idols. The Israelites partook of all the pleasures offered by the women, and their gifts. The same happened repeatedly whenever they encountered other tribes. God demanded mass executions of the idol-worshippers, and Moses obliged by having thousands of Israelites killed. Moses was a law-giver and deliverer of his people, but he also was responsible for the killings of thousands. Some Israelites approached Moses and complained that he was raising himself above all the others. He immediately had them burnt alive. Richard Dawkins suggests that he was not a good role model. When his sister, Miriam, complained to him that he should not have married outside his Faith, God was supposed to have inflicted her with leprosy. There are many inconsistencies. At one stage God wanted to kill Moses because he was not circumcised, yet He protected him when he was accused for marrying outside his Faith. God had allowed them to take large amounts of gold with them when they left Egypt. It was very easy to construct idols with the gold while there was little else to do with it in the desert. It was like giving a man drugs and telling him not to use them.

Moses received the Ten Commandments after spending forty days and nights on the mountain top at Sinai. When he brought the two tablets down he saw that his people had been worshipping the golden calf. Even his brother Aaron was participating. He threw the tablets down, thus breaking them, and chastised his people for their errant ways. He then had to return to the mountain top for another forty days in order to receive a second edition. It appears that the light from God was so powerful that he had to cover his face and eyes. I am told that is why Jews have to cover their heads in the Temple in order to protect themselves from the light of God; covering of their eyes would be impractical.

The Levis who were the priests had a particularly hard time complaining about their conditions. They complained about the leadership of Moses and they said that they would not listen to him. God finally caused them and all their families and all their property to be swallowed into the earth by means of a large sink-hole.

God did not want this disobedient crowd to reach the Promised Land. He did not even want Moses and Aaron to reach the Promised Land. Aaron helped build the golden calf and Moses defied God at Meriba. The settlers of this Land would have to be a new breed, a different generation, fighters, builders, believers in the future – not a band of weary, thankless, unruly idol-worshipping grumbling ex-slaves. They were not fit to take control of a new land; they had no back-bone. However their children were a new generation who had not suffered the trials and tribulations of their parents. They would be better settlers, better fighters and, perhaps, more disciplined.

During his wanderings through the desert Moses received a visit from Jethro, his wife and two children. One visit from his family in forty years does not sound as though they were a doting family, caring for each other and wanting to do things together. However Jethro had

had a great influence on him. He gave Moses sound advice in the Desert, suggesting to him how to contain an unruly mob which was constantly demanding to return to Egypt. Rather a slave in Egypt, they said, where the next meal and a roof over their heads was always available! He taught him methods of organization and introduced him into many Midianite teachings which were added into Israelite ritual. Jethro advised Moses to appoint and to teach the law to other reliable people who could take over the judgments in disputes of lesser importance so that he would not be bothered with every minor complaint, and would have more time for really important matters.

Moses then appointed Joshua to become the leader of the Israelites after he died. From Paran, at the northern end of the desert, twelve spies (one from each tribe) were sent in to Jericho in order to see if it was possible to conquer the land. When the spies returned ten of them said that it would be impossible to take over Jericho. Only Joshua and Caleb gave a positive report. On this report Jericho was later surrounded and conquered, but not until after the death of Moses.

When they arrived at Mount Nebo Moses climbed to the top of the mountain and saw the Promised Land stretched out before him – a land to which he had brought his people after a forty year journey consisting of hardship and suffering, but a land he would never enter. A slap in the face to the law-giver, the man who rescued the Jewish race! He had even asked God to change His mind, but his request was denied. He died at the age of 120 – a prophet, a leader, a savior of the Israelites. He had been present at the death of his brother Aaron. He outlived his sister, his wife and his two sons.

Out of this undisciplined mob that migrated from Egypt the Jewish people became a nation, and, after three millennia, still exist today while other contemporary nations have vanished.

This super-human effort of transplanting an entire nation was accomplished by Moses, born of Hebrew parents, according to the Bible. Yet, never having been circumcised meant that he had never entered into a covenant with God. Circumcision is obviously very important to God, for why else would he have made a covenant with Abraham and then wanted to kill Moses whom he had appointed as a leader of his people?

We have attributed the writing of the Torah to Moses, but this can never be proved. One thing we do know is that he fought for justice. When an Egyptian was seen fighting a Hebrew he fought on the side of the Hebrew, and killed the Egyptian. When Midianite shepherds tried to prevent Jethro's daughters from watering their livestock he protected the daughters from abuse. When God was upset about the grumbling and idolatry of the Hebrews he told Moses that he wished to destroy them as a nation. Moses, who, also had fought with his people about these matters, said to God "Then blot me out, too." "Why", he asked God, "would you bring them all this way only to destroy them after almost forty years of struggle?" Sometimes one wonders as to who was the wiser. Yet he was a flawed and reluctant leader, which makes him more human. He was not always popular with the people, and also he had his arguments with God. He saved and protected his people, but he also killed many. Often, he had to wear two hats – one when he was working with God and one when he was protecting his people –a difficult job to defend both sides at the same time!

Are we saying that the Passover seder is based on mythology since there is no historical or archaeological evidence for the liberation of enslaved Jews in Egypt? It is possible that the whole story is allegorical and taken from numerous incidents having occurred amongst other nations at different times. Yet it teaches a good lesson and gives people a moral by which to live. Apparently people require a belief to give them faith and help them to keep striving. Imagine how unhappy Rose Kennedy would have been if she did not believe that her sons, Jack and Robert, were walking with Jesus in Heaven. Don't you think that the American Civil Rights Movement looked upon the Rev. Martin Luther King as a modern day Moses!

Purim, too, might be a festival that has no real foundation. We read the Book of Esther at that time. Apparently this book tells an ancient children's story which is well known to Iranian children. The name of God is never mentioned in the Book of Esther, unlike all the other Books of the Bible where God's name is repeated numerous times. Persian history makes no mention of a Jewish Queen Esther. The Festival of Purim might have been added as a 'feel-good' story.

Freud wrote "Moses and Monotheism" towards the end of his life, starting it in Germany and completing it in England after he left Germany before World War II. He was an atheist, but the subject of Moses interested him. He says that Moses, the Egyptian, learnt monotheism from Akhnetan, and taught it to the Jews whom he rescued from slavery. Freud maintains that the Jews finally killed Moses, their rescuer. They felt guilty after his death, and developed the concept of the Messiah in order to bring Moses back to them. The guilt of the murder of Moses has been inherited by the Jews, and it is this guilt that drives them to religion which makes them feel better in themselves.

If we did not have a hero in true flesh and blood perhaps we created one with words and dreams and repetition of the same old story. Moses might have been the dream that a struggling people required to bolster their ego while fighting off their enemies and trying to exist for the last three and a half millennia.

CHAPTER 5

Women

Might is right! The strong will overpower the weak. Men, by their muscular advantage due to biiochemical differences, are usually stronger than women. The testosterone hormone gives men an edge in physical strength, making them usually more powerful than their female counterparts. This quirk of nature has given them the ability to hold women down. Ever since the beginning of time the male has dominated the female. He would eat the largest and the tastiest parts of the slain animal, leaving the less desirable and puny portion to his female partner; he would take the best of everything for himself while she would have to be content with the remnants. She began to understand that this was how things would be, and she even made sure that her man would receive the best. This is the norm, she was brought up to believe, and she even encouraged masculine dominance and was proud of her man's strength and status. She aided and abetted the man who was holding her down. We have seen this in the Stockholm Syndrome where the kidnapped subject does all in her power to please and protect her jailer and defend him from outside attacks.

Of course, this male dominance was continued in all aspects of life throughout the millennia that followed. It occurred in religious practice, in politics, in government, in business, in payment of salaries and wherever man wished it to occur. Disparate salaries between the sexes may be because of the lesser or inferior jobs being handed out to women, but when women do equal work they usually do not get equal pay. When women are given more difficult jobs men frequently move out of those jobs to higher levels. It is not unlike the situation when black families move into white areas the white people move elsewhere, perhaps to the northern suburbs. Women were always regarded as the creative source of human life. They were allowed to lead in matters of food preparation, the upbringing of children, maintaining the home and minor family matters – only if the man allowed it, and he usually did as he did not wish to be bothered with small matters especially when he was resting at home after a day's hunting or constructing or other hard and important work.

Governments and corporation boards in almost all cases are grossly under-represented by women. There appears to be a glass ceiling above which women cannot achieve greater heights. They are also discriminated against if they have a child while they are on the work force as they seldom get remunerated for the time that they have to take off from work in order to care for the baby in the important early part of the child's life.

During more recent times, in more modern and liberal countries women have been fighting for their rights and are arriving at a certain amount of success. Total equality has not yet been achieved. Salaries for the female sex have improved in the United States; there are more women on corporate boards and in government in the last few years, although in the majority of cases they have still not achieved parity in financial compensation. However, in most other countries of the world women have probably not yet reached the levels gained in the US. Yet even in the US where gains have been made they are still not enough.

Throughout many areas of the world women are kidnapped or promised good jobs in different countries only to find out when they get there that they have been sold into sex slavery. Their work is to supply sexual favors for the purpose of bringing income to a handful of mobsters. Their lives have been ruined, and they have very little opportunity of getting out of the trap into which they have been led. Disease is rampant and very easily spread.

India, surprisingly, is a country that has had a female prime minister, Indira Gandhi - the daughter of Pandit Jawaharlal Nehru, the first

Prime Minister of India (of course, the name Gandhi would always help in India, even though she was not related to the Mahatma). India has also had a female President – Pratibha Patil. The leader of the Congress Party, Sonia Gandhi, too, is of the female sex. Yet India as a country does not respect women. Apart from Saudi Arabia India is considered the worst country in the world for a woman to grow up.

Indian women are expected to be obedient and walk behind their husbands. Widows may not re-marry. Women are frequently raped, manhandled and treated with disrespect while little punishment is meted out to the perpetrators. If the dowry is not forthcoming from their parents they are divorced or thrown out. When an Indian woman gives birth to a daughter she is cursed, disrespected, shunned by her husband's family and frequently has to seek residence with other such outcasts who have been guilty of the same crime – producing a female child! Thus there are many street corner shops with ultra-sound machines where a woman can find out the sex of the fetus in her womb. If it is a girl she can have an abortion thus saving herself from embarrassment and becoming an outcast. At this rate we will soon notice a preponderance of men in India with an insufficient supply of women for wives. Already it has been seen that there are insufficient women available for marriage, and in some cases there have been men who have lent their wives out to brothers or friends for the purpose of pro-creation.

In Indian families the woman frequently eats last after she has fed the family. She usually eats that which has been left over by her family rather quickly because she has to clean up and perform other tasks in the house. Therefore often she is malnourished. This malnourished woman supplies inadequate nutrition to the baby in her womb when she becomes pregnant giving rise to a stunted infant who starts life with an uphill battle ahead of him. There is a higher percentage of malnutrition in India than in almost any other country in the world.

Facilities for water-borne sewerage are not always available in India. Millions of people have to perform their toilet functions in the open air. Thus defecation and urination are frequently performed in the open air in fields, along railway tracks and behind trees. When women go outside to perform these functions – and sometimes they go in groups in the dark - they are often spied upon by waiting men who have witnessed them in the past (habits are frequently performed at the same time daily), and are raped.

In some ways it is surprising to find that women are treated so poorly in India as women have been revered in the Kama Sutra, in literature and in their mythology and religion. The women are frequently beautiful, and higher caste women are often exceptionally well dressed in their saris and facial make-up.

In Saudi Arabia women are not permitted to drive a car. They cannot open a bank account without their husband's permission. They have no voting rights – yet men who do have voting rights never get a chance to vote, anyhow. They may not wear clothes or make-up that might show off their beauty. They may be arrested if they show too much flesh or make-up. High-heel shoes, too, may stimulate the male by the click they make on the pavement on walking or by the femininity displayed, and are therefore forbidden. They wear the hijabs over their heads and faces, thus leaving very little of their facial features exposed. The Koran does not imply that the hijab must be worn. It merely says that the woman must dress modestly and keep a veil over her bosom; she should not laugh in public. A woman dare not be seen in public with a man who is not her husband, father or member of the family, or else the morality police will arrest her. Even if a husband and wife are together in public they could be requested by the morality police to show proof of marriage.

King Abdullah, in order to save his own skin in the face of critical world opinion, was forced to open up a co-educational university. The result is that more women than men attend the university. In fact, female graduates outnumber male graduates. Yet almost all the post-graduate jobs are given to men. Women are expected to stay at home and take care of their husbands and the children. Obviously Saudi Arabia does not produce soap operas and sit-coms, but these are imported from Turkey and other lands. They are extremely popular with Saudi women, and act as a rare source of pleasure to their dull and unproductive lives, and give them 'food for thought'.

In cases of rape the victim may be charged as she must have stimulated the man to have done what he did. In Shariah Law, such women are sometimes stoned. I have yet to hear of a man being stoned when he has perpetrated a rape.

On account of the high oil revenues gasoline is very cheap. The government doles out large sums of money to the people so there is general satisfaction and therefore very few people speak against the government. There is zero tolerance for those who do speak against the government.

If a woman receives inheritance she can only get one-half of what a man in the family would receive. In Yemen a woman is considered to be only a half of a witness in the courts. She may not leave the house without a man's permission.

Generally, women have been supportive of the democratic processes that brought about the civic disturbances of the Arab Spring, but the democratic movements in the Middle East seem to have fizzled out in Egypt, Libya and Bahrain. At this time there is a prolonged civil war in Iraq, Syria and Yemen while Libya is in an anarchic state being ruled by rival militia groups. So far nothing seems to have been achieved from these democratic uprisings. In fact, the Middle East is entering into a period of greater turmoil. Women have not received any improvement in their civil rights.

Jihadi fighters for ISIS (Islamic State of Iraq and Syria) have been known to kidnap women and line them up like cattle for the purpose of examining them for their virginity. Those who pass the test are taken as wives for producing further fighters for jihad, and those who fail are sold into prostitution.

Let us consider the role of women in the Jewish religion. God, it will be remembered, made a covenant with Abraham that all men of the Chosen People must be circumcised. Abraham circumcised himself at the age of 99. God made no covenant with women. There is no sign to distinguish a woman as a Jewess. God did not ask the women to play any role in the religion. Women are not expected to attend the synagogue, nor is it written that they need to pray. If they do attend the temple they are given a back-seat in a separate insignificant area of the synagogue, away from the men. Covering of their heads is not ordained. The religion, it seems, was intended for the men.

The Bible mentions the names of numerous men who contributed to the history of the Jews whereas in comparison only a few women are named. We are introduced to women through their relationships to their men, such as Lot's wife or Lot's daughters, all of whom play important roles, but we are never given their names. Cain had a son who is named, but who was his wife? In the Bible we read of women begetting sons, but we never read of them begetting daughters. Women are meant to stay at home and care for their men and children. In Ezekial women are told to grieve for the dead because that is what they are good at. A woman has no equal rights in a marriage. If she wants to be divorced from her husband she can only get a divorce from him if he wishes to do so; without a 'get' (divorce) she can never re-marry. The ex-husbands are frequently spiteful.

Women were never admitted into the priesthood not only because they had insufficient education and were not required to pray but also because they were considered impure as a result of their menstrual cycles and childbirth. They are considered impure for long periods following childbirth, even more so after the birth of a girl than a boy, and they have to de-contaminate anything that they might have touched during that period.

The mikveh is a ritual pool indoors and filled with at least 200 gallons of rain water. All women, following menstruation and childbirth have to immerse themselves completely in order to purify their bodies and souls. Before entering the mikvah the woman must wash her body thoroughly. In the case of menstruation she must enter the mikveh one week later, and must not have sexual relations with her husband until after she has been 'purified'. Until a menstruating woman has been to the mikveh she is considered dirty.

The daily morning prayer recited by men includes the passage "Thank God that I was not born a woman". In Biblical times they were considered to be the property of men. They were denied education. Their testimony was not acceptable in court. They were considered to be necessary for procreation, otherwise men should keep away from them – especially foreign women who were referred to as vixens and nymphomaniacs.

Deuteronomy 22 states that if you find a virgin and seize her you have to pay her father in silver. No sympathy for the young lady, but you have shamed her father! The woman who has been raped is forced to marry her rapist and has to live with him forever! There is no sensitivity or understanding for the woman.

Jeremiah 44, 24 "I said to all the people and all the women". Men are people, and women are something else! Josephus, the Jewish historian turned Roman, said that authority was given by God to men, and therefore women should remain silent.

Truly, there were some women in the Bible who were leaders, such as Deborah who was one of the Judges. She led her people into battle. There is the story of Esther, Queen of Persia, who saved her people from a cruel Jew-hater. However, some authorities consider this as just a story since the history of Persia does not confirm such a Queen as having existed. This might be a borrowed tale introduced for the 'feel good' effect.

The Christian Church also discriminates against women. Women cannot become priests or hold high positions in the Catholic and Protestant Churches. Lately, however, some minor changes have been allowed in certain congregations. In the 4th century St Jerome announced that women led men to the gate of the Devil, the path of wickedness and had the effect of the sting of a serpent. Thomas Aquinas in the 13th century said that women performed a unique role in conception, but at work a man would be better assisted by other men. St Paul felt that women should be quiet in church, and that if they had a problem they should discuss it with their husbands at home. St. Augustine said that the woman's role was limited to procreation.

Yet Jesus was very kind and friendly to women. He treated them as equals. He befriended Mary Magdalene. She stood by him to the end. She was there at his crucifixion and she was the one who found his body missing on the Sunday in the cave where he had been placed after he was brought down from the Cross. However in earlier days when a Canaanite woman asked Jesus for help to cure her child he answered that he was not about to take the bread away from the children to feed the dogs! Alien non-Jewish women were often referred to as dogs.

Towards the onset of Christendom women were treated better than they were treated in the Old Testament, but towards the Middle Ages their role deteriorated. The male was the dominant figure and could pray to God while she was his inferior, having been created from man's rib. The titles for the leaders of the Church were taken from the names of the men – Father, Abbot (from the Hebrew 'father' – 'abba') and Pope (from Papa). Women played no role in the hierarchy of the Church.

The African continent was less affected by events in Europe, but the trend is the same, stressing the inferiority of women. Female genital mutilation is practiced in Africa and the Middle East. It probably originally came from the African tribesmen because there is no mention of this in the Koran even though Muslims in Africa, Yemen and some areas of Saudi Arabia participate in this ritual which was probably learnt from African tribesmen. It is a widespread rite, and it is estimated that about 150 million women have been affected by this practice. It is usually performed between the ages of four and eight. Now that Muslim immigration to Europe has increased the practice of genital mutilation has arrived there with it. It is illegal in most European countries, but the police are usually inexperienced in searching for this sort of crime. Genital mutilation involves removal of some of the external sex organs and sewing up the aperture, allowing a small hole for the drainage of urine and menstrual flow. In some countries, such as Eritrea and the lands in the Horn of Africa, the mutilation is even more extreme. Infibulation, or the removal of the entire external sexual apparatus is performed in those countries. The procedure is usually done by a woman, midwife or barber without anesthesia under unsterile conditions. Infection, hemorrhage, cyst formation and chronic pain frequently follow. Sometimes the women remain infertile. The purpose apparently is to prevent pre-marital sex or any pleasure derived from it. When the woman marries the sutured area is opened up. Difficulties in childbirth may result. If a woman at marriage is found not to have been genitally mutilated, she risks being scorned and looked down upon. So it seems that genital circumcision carries with it a high social status for those who have had it done as compared to those who have not been through the procedure.

Obviously female circumcision is a more complicated procedure and a far more serious matter than male circumcision – another situation showing male dominance!

What of the status of women in a highly developed society such as the United States? By modern standards it, too, is shameful. Our Founding Fathers said "All men are born equal". They did not say "All men and women are born equal" and they obviously did not include black men and slaves as many of the Founding Fathers were slave-owners. For centuries now women have not received equal pay for equal labor, nor have they been encouraged to join certain professions. It was as late as about 1920 when women were first allowed to vote, and then only after numerous demonstrations and marches and fights. There were terrible fights, both physical and verbal, and numerous arrests. Even though there are improvements in the lot of women there is still a long way to go. They hold far fewer leadership roles in business and government.

Yet women in the US today feel free and enjoy more liberties than their counterparts in most countries of the world. They are not tied to the house as they used to be and they are joining the work force in larger numbers. With advances in birth control measures they are able to plan their children's births to occur at times which would be suitable for them. Through the Affordable Health Care Act contraceptives can be received without cost.

Women earn less than men for similar jobs, and the disparity is even greater in women of color. White women doing the same work, at best, earn about 75% of men's salaries. However, the lower salaries tend to improve as time goes by. Leadership positions for women have also been low down on the scale, but are improving. Women's role in the professions have greatly increased and spread in many different fields.

Modern China appears to have done much towards elevating the status of women. Before the Communist revolution marriage was really between two families, not between two individuals. Marriages were arranged so that the families would receive benefit from the alliance of two people – either it was good for business or for the family tradition. The woman had few rights, being considered as though she was like property owned by the husband. After the Revolution laws which gave the woman a say in her marriage were enacted. She was allowed equality and even earned the right to divorce. In the past men had concubines, but today if a woman is aware that her husband has other wives or concubines she can exercise her rights. There is a law that there should be only one child per family so as to keep the rising population numbers down, but it does not specify the sex of the child.

Man is essentially a bully. He has proved this throughout history. He has taken advantage of his strength. He has killed animals first for food, and then for sport. Animal skins, skulls, tusks and horns are collected and sold at a high price or displayed with pride to announce one's heroism to the world. Many species of animals have been extinguished or are almost extinct. Man has killed animals for sport. What kind of a sport is it when the animal has no weapon and is exposed out in the open while man is hiding and is armed with a big gun? He has made weaker or unarmed men his slaves and forced them to do his labor in order to increase his own wealth. He has conquered weaker nations so he could have their land and minerals and gold and oil, and has proceeded to collect taxes from them. He has decimated populations because he did not like the color of their skin or their religion. In many instances he has sent his children into battle to fight his wars and kill for him. And, as we have seen, he has subjected his mate – the mother of his children – to a lowly status and to serve his needs.

So what are we as a civilized 21ˢᵗ century world doing today about the inequality of the sexes? Silence pervades. Religion and the interpretation of the Bible frequently prevent the victims from receiving the civil rights to which they are entitled. Power and long-lasting habits and traditions help to maintain the status quo. But where is the outcry? Are men so comfortable with their superior status that they will do nothing or very little to right these obvious wrongs? The world permits genital mutilation to millions of African and Middle Eastern young girls to continue. Rapes occurring in the Congo and the surrounding lands - said to be thousands every day – are allowed to persist as though they were perfectly normal events, and nobody ever is apprehended! If an unaccompanied woman in a Muslim country complains about having been raped and can prove who the rapist was, she may receive lashes or another punishment for having been out of the house without a male guardian.

We have advanced in science and technology but our ethics and morals in the treatment of women remain in the Dark Ages.

CHAPTER 6

Witch-Doctors

Witch-doctors are neither witches nor doctors. They protect their patients against witches and they treat them through ancestral spirits. They usually add herbal remedies to the cure; these usually are derived from plant-life, and to this occasionally could be added portions of animals and insects.

A witch-doctor in Africa is known as a sangoma or, in some areas, as an umtagati. A doctor who has a Western-oriented education is referred to as an inyanga. Witch-doctors will tell you that they have within them, or they are in communication with a spirit of a bygone ancestor which gives them the ability of performing their healing functions. Some will tell you that their ancestors have called upon them to follow in this particular calling. Ancestors and their spirits play a predominant role in the beliefs of the Bantu peoples of Southern Africa, more so than deities. Ancestors are believed to control the lives of their people on earth; their influence may reach even further, such as the weather and the future!

A sangoma, unlike his Western-educated medical counterpart, does not specialize in any particular field. He is a generalist. He or she – there are numerous female sangomas as well – performs physical and spiritual healing, administers herbal medicines known as 'muti', exorcises evil influences, and enacts rituals such as those required in births, deaths, marriages and entrance into adulthood. In some ways sangomas are like priests and rabbis, as when they practice and teach the tribal traditions.

They resemble teachers when they pass on the history of their people. They are also fortune tellers. If a tribesman has lost a valuable possession or some of his cattle he might go to see his witch-doctor in order to try to re-possess the missing articles or animals. Witch-doctors can predict rain and changes in the weather; they may call upon their ancestors to produce rain in seasons of drought. At any time they may contact and converse with their ancestral spirits for advice on how to perform certain deeds.

Witch-doctors respect the ancestors of the people, and they show their feelings by chanting, dancing, throwing of the bones and drum-beating. They also interpret the traditions, history and rituals of their people. Sometimes they read the positions of the stars in the sky and explain certain celestial phenomena in their own inimitable ways. Even though they are the ones who throw the bones they will tell you that it is the departed ancestors who interpret the meaning of where and how the bones lie, and it is they that pass on the information to the witch-doctor.

When a sick African needs help he will immediately turn to his witch-doctor, the person who has healed him and his family in the past.

In many African countries the work of the witch-doctors is considered legal. Many of the large gold and diamond mines in South Africa employ witch-doctors because the majority of the miners who come from rural districts from within the country and the surrounding lands have always gone to witch-doctors for their health and other problems, and have never been to a Western-trained medical person. Others first try a witch-doctor, and only when he has not been successful do they visit a conventional doctor. In the beginning they usually do not trust the Western-trained physician. Only with time and experience will they later respect the work done for them by the physician, but they will never forget the witch-doctor to whom they will one day return.

Those who have received the calling from an ancestral spirit usually undergo an apprenticeship with a more senior sangoma for many months or a few years before they go out alone into their own private practices.

One can easily understand the need for a witch-doctor by primitive man. There were enough physical phenomena, such as floods, hurricanes and earth-quakes against which there was no relief. Also, there were physical ailments – diseases, infections, suffering and pain, and death – where man was helpless. Enter the witch-doctor who brought confidence, help from ancestors, and sometimes relief. Here was another hero!

Once while I was still a resident at the Baragwaneth Hospital back in South Africa I was called in the middle of the night to see a new admission. He was a Black man, sweating and in obvious pain. I set about taking a history before I examined him.

"Where is the pain?" I asked him.

"Everywhere" he responded.

"Is it in your head or your belly or your chest or your arms and legs?" I tried to get some information.

"Everywhere. I told you already" he insisted.

"Can you describe the pain?" I enquired while trying to maintain my equilibrium. "Is it sharp like a knife or does it burn you or is it a throbbing pain?"

He was getting annoyed with me. "Why must you ask me these questions? I am sick. You can see that! My umtagati at home does not ask me any questions. He can see what is wrong with me just by looking at me and in my eyes. Then he gives me muti, and then I am fine." Muti is medicine.

History-taking was obviously redundant in this case. I proceeded to listen to his chest. It was as still as the grave. "Take a deep breath" I called. His breath sounds were very hard to hear through his thick chest wall.

"Take a deep breath" I called out again. There was no response.

I said it in his language. "Pefe. Pefe mula." "Breathe. Breathe deeply".

"I am too tired to pefe" he explained. "My umtagati does not examine me or ask me to pefe".

"Well, I am not your umtagati. I am your doctor, and this is the way I examine and treat you" I flashed back.

"You should go and learn from the umtagati".

So it was when a new patient who had never been to a Western-trained physician arrived in our hospital. Once even I had the occasion to call upon a witch-doctor for assistance. It happened many years ago while I was working as a doctor on a large mine in Randfontein, South

Africa. As I was the Senior Medical Officer to the mine I was given the house adjacent to the hospital in which to live. We had a servant, Selena, to help my wife take care of the house and the children. She had been with us for a few years.

One morning, as I was getting ready to go to work Selena walked into the kitchen and said to me "Doctor, please give me my money because I have to leave this job."

Taken aback, I said "Do you mean that you wish to leave us?"

When she answered yes, I asked her why she wanted to go.

"You have a tokolos in this house!" she stated. A tokolos, amongst the Bantu population in South Africa, is an evil spirit which has to be taken seriously. A tokolos may cause havoc. It may be responsible for illness and even death. The harm done is unpredictable. The word mentioned amidst a group of Black people is greeted ominously. All fear the tokolos!

I tried to tell her that she must be imagining the presence of the tokolos as nobody had ever reported the presence of one in this house before, but it was of no avail. I gave her the money owed to her and she went on her way. She was soon replaced, but after a few days the new servant came to me, and said "I cannot stay here any longer, please give me my pay and let me go".

When I asked her why she wanted to leave, she said "I cannot live with this tokolos here."

I was beginning to feel uncomfortable while harboring a tokolos on my premises. Yet I tried again. A new young lady arrived the next day, but the same fate was in store for us. Instead we felt that perhaps we should invite a male to work for us. He might be more stoic, and might handle the problem more philosophically. Within the next day or two a very pleasant young man arrived to work for us. For about two days all was quiet. One afternoon I returned from work in the midst of a drenching tropical thunder-storm. Looking through the window I vaguely discerned a man standing under a large tree in front of the house. I opened the window and saw that it was our new employee.

I shouted out to him "John, don't stand there. You could be struck by lightning. Go to your room or come into the kitchen!"

"I will not go into my room. I want to leave this job" he responded.

When I questioned him as to why he wished to terminate his job he replied (you guessed it!) "It is because you have a tokolos!"

I obviously had a tokolos, and I did not know what to do about it. I decided to call my friend, George Holl. He was the mine manager, and he knew a great deal about the Bantu people as he employed twenty thousand of them on the mine.

"George" I said, "I have a tokolos. What can I do about it?" I explained the situation to him.

"I will send you a witch-doctor" he said. "He will get rid of it. We employ a number of them on the mine. They are kept very busy. Some of our miners will not go to anyone else. I will send one out to you tomorrow morning."

"Does he do house calls?" I asked.

"He will do anything I ask him to."

The next morning a witch-doctor rang my door-bell. Dressed in full regalia, bedecked in ostrich feathers, small animal bones and bells tinkling from his belt as he moved, he asked me to tell him about my problem. I told him that we had a tokolos.

"Take me to the servant's quarters" he requested.

I led him to the room at the back of the property where the servants resided. He walked inside, looked around and came outside. "Yes, you have a big tokolos" was his final decision.

He then set about doing his job. He chanted and raged; he sang and danced; he threw the bones and rolled in the sand. The sun was beating down on him, but he continued running in and out of the room, shouting and making animal sounds. He sweated profusely and appeared to be exhausted. After about a half an hour of heavy work he announced "The tokolos is gone."

I thanked him for his efforts and paid him his fee. The next day we employed a young woman to work in our house. She was cheerful and performed all her duties without any complaint. She stayed for a few years until she got married. We never heard the word 'tokolos' again."

I had another encounter with a witch-doctor. My Auntie Annie was a sick woman. She had heart trouble, diabetes and difficulty in breathing, as well as arthritis. She was always visiting her doctors, taking multiple medications, and showing very little improvement. She was becoming depressed and disgusted with herself.

One day she said to her husband "Please drive me to Pretoria. I believe there is a very good witch-doctor there. He has helped many people. Maybe he can help me, too".

"Are you crazy?" asked Uncle Isaac. "If the specialists in Johannesburg can't help you, how do you expect to get relief from an ignorant witch-doctor?"

"They say that he is very good. I would like to try him" she insisted.

"This is ridiculous! Do you think a savage can outdo these university professors" Uncle Isaac ranted." Ask Sidney, and he will tell you the same."

I was considered the final arbiter of all things medical. I had recently graduated from Medical School and I was supposed to know everything. They approached me and asked me if I thought it was a good idea for her to visit this witch-doctor. I certainly had no faith in voodoo medicine, but wishing to be tactful I answered "Well, what have you got to lose since she is not getting any better?"

"I will only take her if you come with us" said Uncle Isaac to me.

I was put into a position where I felt that I had to go with them. We set out for Pretoria, about forty miles away, early in the morning. While driving my uncle kept on complaining constantly about this trip we were making. "We could be home doing something useful", and "I can't believe that you think this idiot can help you" and "From which beer hall do you think he graduated?"

Suddenly we heard a bang and realized that we had a punctured tire. Now Uncle Isaac and I set about replacing the spare tire for the damaged one. You can imagine the curses that emitted from his mouth at this stage. "We should never have left for this insane adventure to visit a nincompoop!"

When the job was done we continued on our way. Finally we arrived at the witch-doctor's home, but there was a long line leading out of his house, stretching to beyond the corner. This too caused explosive remarks from my precious uncle. After a long and slow advance of the queue we were pleased to be inside the cool house. We looked across the room and saw the witch-doctor sitting on the floor under the window. Slowly he stood up and walked across the room towards us. He was dressed in full regalia, with the ostrich feathers and the bones. He stopped in front of Uncle Isaac.

"Get out of my house!" he called to him. "You have been cursing me for many days now. Even today you have been insulting me. I don't want to look at your ugly face. Now get out!"

Uncle Isaac was astounded. He could not believe what he had heard. Nor could we! As he was walking out the witch-doctor said to Auntie Annie "You can stay. You are very sick" and to me "You must help her."

Then he said to her "Your blood is very sweet, and your heart forgot how to pump the blood. The room is full of air, but you don't know how to breathe it, and you have no oil in your joints."

I thought that just about summed up Auntie Annie's condition, despite the fact that he asked her for no history and did not examine her. He just looked in her eyes. It was almost as good as a diagnostician's report. He went ahead and made a concoction from some bottles of what looked like roots and tiny insects, and placed the combination in a cup with a lid on it.

With this he approached Auntie Annie and said "Take one teaspoon of this muti when the sun is over there", and he pointed eastward, "and one teaspoon when the sun is over there", and he pointed up above, "and one teaspoon when the sun is there", and he pointed to the west. "When it is all finished come and see me again, but don't let that ugly man drive you here. I will not look at him again".

He appeared to be adamant on that point. During the next week Auntie Annie took her muti religiously, and she swore that she had not felt so well in a long time. Unfortunately she passed away before the week ended.

I can remember one other incident involving a witch-doctor. When I was a young lad my mother used to have the seder which was the commencement of the festival of Passover at our home. She invited all members of the family which amounted to about twenty-five to thirty people. The seder consists of a meal commemorating the Biblical story of the Jews under the leadership of Moses escaping from Egypt where they had been slaves unto Pharaoh. This meal is accompanied by the recitation, steeped in tradition, of the events at that time and their forty year journey through the desert. Included are commentaries from various authorities. It is a celebration of the end of slavery for the Jews. There is a time towards the end of the evening ritual when a glass is filled with wine and left at the end of the table. The front door is opened for Elijah, the prophet, to enter and drink the wine. Of course, he does not enter, and then the door is closed.

I had an uncle in those days who was known as a practical joker. On the morning of the seder, while he was in the city he went into the home of a witch-doctor and spoke to him. He asked him if he would do him a favor and come to our house (he wrote the address on a piece of paper) at about 10 p.m. in his full costume; then he was to wait outside the front door. Soon after ten o'clock the front door would be opened; he would enter the house and see many people sitting around the table; he would find a glass of wine at the end of the table closest to the front door. He was to drink the wine rapidly and hastily leave the house. For this my uncle would pay him a considerable sum.

That evening we all sat around the tables at the seder eating and drinking the wine and reciting the ritual passages. Some were beginning to doze from the wine and, perhaps, from boredom as it took a few hours to complete the service. Then we came to the time when the glass was filled for Elijah and the opening of the front door.

Suddenly a man with a mask over his face, with ostrich feathers coming out of his hat, and bells ringing from his belt came rushing into the room, stopped at the first table, grabbed the glass of wine, drank it down to the last drop, and ran out of the house. Everybody stared disbelievingly at what might have been an apparition. All were agog; nobody said a word. After a minute or two elapsed laughter broke out as realization dawned. This must have been the first time that the prophet Elijah was present at a seder!

Yes, there seems to be a place for witch-doctors in Africa. They fulfill a duty, in some cases better than the Western-oriented physician.

CHAPTER 7

The Whistle-Blower

They said that I should speak up and not hide the truth. They said that if you allow a monster to get away with murder you are as guilty as he is. You are aiding and abetting him. If you know that a murderer is lying, especially since the people whose lives he has taken are not there to defend themselves, stand up for justice and human rights. Don't be a coward! We will all benefit from it if you open your mouth and give evidence against the evil person. I believed that they were right. I felt it in by bones and I spoke up. I knew that I could make a difference. I did this for the sake of human rights and for justice, and to defend the voiceless and lifeless who are no longer with us, and their grieving loved ones. Today I wish that I had not listened to them and that I had never interfered. I could have had a normal life like most other people. All I achieved was a life of misery – hell on earth! – and no thanks from anyone.

I was born and lived in a land where I was very happy. I grew up in a middle class family. My father earned a good living working as an accountant and my mother was a school teacher. I was considered bright at my school work and I was a naturally talented athlete. I played in the school teams and excelled as a sprinter. I went to university and graduated as a lawyer. While at college I met the love of my life; she, too, became a lawyer at the same time as I did. We married, and since we were both enthusiastic about our professions we decided not to have any children until at least the time would arrive when we will have established ourselves in our practices.

A happy and quiet life was soon turned into turmoil as a military coup overthrew our government and ousted the leaders of our country. There was nothing we could do about it except hope and pray that things would settle down and life would return to normality. Our rosy hopes were soon demolished when we realized that we were living under a despotic dictatorship. The newspapers became government-controlled. They told us only of the great strides we were making as a nation, how our crop production had never been so great, how crime was down and how happy our people were. Yet all the faces we looked upon in the streets were glum, and those of us who listened in secretly to short-wave radio stations from outside the country heard of the round-up of political prisoners in our own country, assassinations of important figures in the old regime and mass killings. This hardly sounded like the same land that our newspapers, radio and television reports were describing. They never told us of those who disappeared in the middle of the night and those who suddenly became fatherless, brotherless and childless. Of course, we did hear about certain people who had disappeared – some had been taken from their beds by the secret police and some just failed to re-appear where they had always been seen, such as at their desks at work or playing with their children in the park. We heard of those who wailed and sobbed because of the loss of a loved one, but we were assured that nothing untoward would happen to us if we only obeyed the laws and did not attempt to be rabble-rousers. The missing ones, we were told, were collected and sent to a highly advanced camp where they were undergoing corrective treatment. They would be home soon – that day never seemed to come.

My wife and I continued with our work but it soon became obvious to us that as a result of the financial depression that settled in throughout the land our office expenses were higher than our earnings, so we decided to close the office. My wife went to work for a large firm of lawyers and I was offered a job with the government, which paid fairly well. It involved legal work which is what interested me as long as I was not involved with the politics of the regime. However, I soon realized that my appointment brought me into daily contact with the right hand man of our president whom we all knew was a dictator. This worried me a little but I knew that my integrity could not be interfered with – and if there was a political problem I would leave. My hands would remain clean.

It did not take long for me to understand that our dictator's right-hand man was a leader of a secret unit known as the Wolfhounds. They would arrest or kill anyone who was considered an enemy of the state, and render others who were less dangerous, harmless by removing documents and weapons from their homes. There was an organized purification of the nation by the Wolfhounds, and my boss was the leader of the pack! However, he did nothing on his own. Everything that was accomplished was first discussed with our dictator in the room adjacent to my office. I can assure you that it was not difficult for me to listen in to what my boss and the dictator were talking about. I am sure that they did not realize that I was able to hear the conversations of their plans through the thin boards that separated our offices. The talks centered on the removal of all forms of possible obstruction to their authority. They said that their goal was to produce a pure unadulterated society. Nobody with any power or any thoughts of opposing the government could hope to survive.

I heard them talking about the Chief of Police one morning. My boss said that he was too soft and too slow about carrying out orders. "Get rid of him" I heard the dictator say. The next day I read that the Chief of Police had committed suicide – their explanation of his assassination! One day I heard them discussing whether a certain high official was an enemy of the government. They were not sure. "Don't take any chances. He must go" answered our brave dictator. It was not long before this suspected individual, too, was gone. I read in the paper that he was run over by a car in the parking lot of the large apartment building where he lived. There were many such examples that I could quote, but what is the point of adding more fuel to the fire? The fire was already burning. Every day I listened in to the list of those who might be dangerous to our Great Dictator. Each morning it was like hearing a new issue of the menu for today's killings. The results were inevitable.

However, I was no longer able to exist in this world of hate and intrigue and planned death. I had to leave my job and seek employment elsewhere. I was fearful that I might be considered to be a suspect by them if I resigned from my job, but I got away intact and apparently without leaving any suspicions behind. I went to work at a different place for less money, but with a clearer conscience.

For many years we lived under this state of Fascism where people feared the knock on the door after midnight and the destructive entry of the Wolfhounds. One fine day we woke up, not suspecting that this day would be different from any other day. Suddenly with the bleating over microphones and announcements over the radio with a fanfare of trumpets we were told that Fascism was over and our dictator was overthrown by a military coup. Our dictator and his henchmen had been arrested during the early hours of the morning. The army promised fair elections in the near future and that a democratic government would be instituted. Despite the dictatorial powers and the Intelligence of the old regime as well as the secret actions of the Wolfhounds our Leader had no idea that the army had been planning a purge.

Our dictator who was on the wanted list by Interpol (international police) was handed over to the International Court of Justice in The Hague. Months elapsed before any trial took place. There was much legal wrangling, but when the trial finally occurred we followed it verbatim in the newspapers as it was printed in full detail all over our land.

He was accused of the slaughter of thousands of citizens without trial. He denied this. He was asked if he knew of the Wolfhounds. Yes, he had heard of them. He was questioned as to whether he had control over their actions, their murders and their lawless attacks on innocent victims. No, he had nothing to do with their abuses of power; they were a bunch of illegal trouble-makers. Was he in favor of their illegal activities? Certainly not, he was out to get them and his intentions were to charge them under the full extent of the law. He was actually hot on their trail when this illegal coup that overthrew him, occurred. He wished that he would only have had enough time to get them before the army took over.

I was sick to my stomach when I read these newspaper reports – our press had become free again - as was everyone else that we knew. I spoke to my wife about these reports; she, too, was devastated. The truth was that nobody could really be absolutely certain that our dictator had been lying. Nobody was coming forward with any evidence against him. We were all more than suspicious, but what proof was there? I had proof. I had worked in the office adjacent to our head of government. I had heard him talking to my boss. I had heard him giving out orders for the Wolfhounds to get rid of numerous individuals. There was no better witness than me!

I was the only person who could probably help to provide a guilty verdict. All our friends said "You've got to go!" If I did not come forward I could never face myself again. I would be complicit with the crime. I would be aiding and abetting a criminal who had been responsible for the deaths of so many of our people. My wife and I spent many nights talking and crying about this. I was not the type of person who could easily come forward on such occasions, but I realized that I must – even for the sake of my own conscience.

We made enquiries through our Foreign Office. I said that I wanted to go to The Hague to give evidence at the trial of our dictator. I told them what information I had. There was much discussion by phone and E-Mail. Then I received a phone call to come and receive my tickets as I was flying to the Netherlands that evening.

I arrived in Amsterdam, and was taken directly to The Hague. I was assured that my testimony would be anonymous, I would be given a number, my voice would be altered and the cameras would not show my face clearly as my face would be blurred on the monitors. I was questioned both by the prosecution and the defense. I described the conversations that I had overheard between our dictator and his henchmen, and I told them about the deaths of the people that they had discussed which I read about in the newspapers – deaths described as accidental. I was even able to display notes and signatures of certain orders that were given by him and which I found on my ex-boss' desk. I noticed the changes in expression on the face of our dictator as I described what I had heard and seen. Until now he had thought that he was getting away with the atrocities that he had committed, but I swung the case in favor of the truth. Justice prevailed, and our dictator was sentenced to many years of imprisonment.

He never served a single day of his sentence because he died before he was to enter into his life of confinement. He had been suffering from a chronic kidney ailment and hypertension. His partners in crime were either given short sentences or were not apprehended. I returned home unaffected by the turn of events, but feeling satisfied that I had done my duty as a citizen, that justice was served. I knew that if I had not spoken up it would have been a victory for evil and civilization would have taken a step backwards. Unfortunately, I discovered later, there was one occasion that my real voice and real face were shown on television in my own country due to a technological error.

I went back home, but it did not take long before I began to realize that I was a target for execution. I had never felt like this before. I had a cold and was not feeling well when I returned from The Hague, so I did not go to work and spent the day at home catching up on some paper work. I saw, looking through my window of our fourth floor apartment, two men keeping an eye on our building. They stayed there all day, and at dusk I watched their replacements arriving; I saw them standing and walking about all night. When I awoke during the night they were still there.

The following day I went to work. As I walked out of the building I noticed these two men following me. I jumped into a cab, which I usually do not use for getting to work. When I arrived at the office I saw these two men getting out of their parked car. I felt very edgy at work all day. When I left my office and walked out of the building onto the street I saw them waiting for me. Again I entered a cab and went home. Once in my building I could see them outside as though they were on military duty.

I discussed the turn of events with my wife. I assured her that this was not a figment of my imagination. She tried to make light of it all, suggesting that it would probably not happen again. However, on the week-end we decided to go out to the country for a picnic. We had to cross the road to get to our car. My wife was a few feet in front of me carrying the hamper and a few other articles. While I was in the middle of the road I glanced to the side to make sure that the road was clear, but I saw a car from seemingly nowhere speeding straight towards me. Instinctively I dived for the sidewalk, and by some miracle I was alive.

I was again severely shaken. By now my wife was convinced that they were out to get me. Before going to bed that night I slowly separated the curtains of my window to see if the two men were still waiting outside. While I was still focusing my eyes on the scene there was a bang and a shattering of glass as a bullet came hurtling into my bedroom. Again, I was lucky to have survived another attempt on my life. My wife peered through the window but the assailants had fled.

"We cannot go on living like this" asserted my wife. "We must do something about it before it is too late. At this rate you will soon be a corpse."

The next day we flew back to the Hague, and we immediately contacted the authorities at the International Court of Justice. We consulted with a group of attorneys there and described how we have been shadowed and followed, and the attempts on our lives There was only one conclusion. We must leave the country of our birth, they told us. We must go and live elsewhere in another country, preferably far away. That is too drastic, we said. We cannot leave our work, our family, our friends.

"But they will follow you to the ends of the earth" suggested one of the attorneys. "They will find out from a friend or a neighbor or a member of your family where you are, and they will kill you. You know to what ends extremists will go! They will stop at nothing! Doing nothing means awaiting an inevitable death."

"You will have to give up your identities. You will have to take on new names, new papers, new passports, new lives. Diplomas and passports and driver's licenses and credit cards are yours no longer. You will have to give up your past lives, and start a new existence in a different country. You must forget the past and never refer to it. You will build a new future."

It was a shock for us to hear this, but we realized that it was the only way to stay alive. The thought of changing our names and giving up our friends, parents and families was scary. It sounded awful, but we had to get away in order to escape, for the meantime, certain death. It was ghoulish to think of having to get out of your body, your past – your life – and get into a new one and start living again. It was easier said than done. The only good thing was that we did not have any children yet.

We decided to come and live in this land, from where I am writing these notes. We drove to the airport at the dead of night, followed by a green car that we managed to shake off at a railroad crossing when we slipped through as the gates were coming down. We left our car at the airport, knowing that we would never return to pick it up again. When the plane departed we realized that this would be the last time that we were using our real names.

We always wanted to visit this country and had decided that one day, when we had enough money, we would come and vacation here. We never thought that we would be vacationing here permanently. We have no complaints about life in this country. Of course, we are living in a cheap apartment that requires a lot of work. We can hardly afford the rent. I feel sick when I remember the gorgeous place we lived in before we came here. I don't know how we will ever sell our place in the old country as our deeds and signatures do not apply to us anymore.

Since we arrived here we have had two children, a boy and a girl. They are normal and healthy children. They speak the language of this land like natives, unlike their parents who have thick accents and are always looked upon as aliens. We often search for words, and it takes a great effort not to use the words of the language which we have spoken so fluently all our lives. Our children cannot understand why their parents speak the language so poorly. They do not know that their parents came from another land.

We have made friends here, but they are not like our friends whom we have had since childhood. Our old friends do not know where we are and why we did not say good-bye. Our children want to know why they have no grandparents. Little do they realize that their grandparents are alive in a land far, far away.

The pain of having parents and friends whom we cannot see or speak to is unbearable. The fact that we cannot even talk to others about them is so unnatural. I sometimes lie in bed and sob like a child. We often feel so cowardly for having run from life. We feel so guilty for not having told our families and friends where we were going. But we feared that there may be some leak and we would be tracked. We feel that we are not normal people – we have no history, no childhood tales to tell, no photographs, no memorabilia. We are people without a past. We are like aliens from outer space who have landed on this planet.

In the old country we both went to college and qualified as attorneys, but we cannot practice law as we dare not show our certification under our original names. Without qualifications or experience in other fields we have had to settle for lesser paying jobs. My wife works in a retail store as a floor manager and I am a cashier in a large grocery store.

I sometimes wonder if it was worthwhile acting as witness against our Great Dictator and suffering the pain and unhappiness that has since befallen us. Our dictator is dead, but that was a result of natural causes – not because of the part I played. No good came from my evidence even though I spent three days on the witness stand. Most of his henchmen escaped trials and punishment; only a few received light sentences. I would not have been hunted nor would I have undergone voluntary self-exile had I kept my mouth shut. I would have lived out the rest of my life as others do. Also, I have caused my wife irreparable harm for which I cannot forgive myself even though she has never complained or blamed me. Because of me she, too, lives like a pariah, cut off from her family and friends.

I did what was expected from me. In more pejorative language, I was a whistle-blower. Whistle-blowers often dig their own graves. While they think that they are doing the right thing for the people other people sometimes look upon them as trouble-makers. I have heard it said that if you do not report a criminal you are aiding and abetting him. Yet nobody has told of what happens to you if you report him. You are urged to take action for the good of the people, but your future is not considered to be of any importance!

I would have been better off if I had not given evidence against the tyrant. I achieved nothing positive, and I ruined my life and the lives of my wife and children. We have lost our parents. Yes, you can say that they are dead, as far as we are concerned. Our parents have lost their children and grandchildren. And to them, we are as good as dead. They don't know our new names or where we are. They don't even know that they are grandparents. They must be mourning the lives of their son and daughter-in-law. They know that if we were alive we would have somehow contacted them. Our university education was for naught – we cannot make use of it. We cannot practice our professions, as our certification must be considered null and void. We are struggling to make ends meet. We feel like criminals hiding our past lives, as though our lives were bathed in sin and crime. We have to lie when questioned about our pasts, and sometimes we have to expand the lies when the queries become deeper. We also have to remember the lies we tell as we will probably be asked the same questions at a later date. Every time that someone asks us something we have to think hard as to how to reply. I am sure we appear to be suspicious-looking characters. Nothing is getting better with time. It seems only to be getting worse.

We live the lives of criminals, even though we are innocent while the real criminals walk around and live the lives of the innocent. Those who have sinned receive the blessings of the just, and we, the just, are living in Hell!

I am in a state of depression and have often wanted to commit suicide. I have no confidence in myself any more. I am afraid to meet people or go anywhere as I might make a slip and say something that I should not or give away some secrets from my past. I must remember that I was born as one particular person, but will die as someone else.

I have gone to visit a psychiatrist. But what was the point of going to improve my mental health when I cannot tell my psychiatrist the truth or even who I am? He knows nothing of my past, except lies, lies, lies that I told him. He wanted to know where I was from since I speak with a foreign accent. I had to lie and say that I got my accent from my parents who came from abroad. He must have thought that I was very strange. I was afraid to go back to him again. He is sure to ask me more questions about the past. Doesn't your present state of mind depend on your past development? How could he treat a liar with no past? There is no future for one who has no past.

Our dictator is dead, but his accomplices are free. I, too, am supposedly free, but I am trapped in my body in a foreign land. I did what my conscience said was the right thing to do, but it was to my own detriment. I made myself a stranger upon this earth. I will never again walk the streets of my own land while the murderous tyrants may do so without a care. Like a martyr I stood up for truth, but it did not bring me to the Promised Land, as I had hoped. It made me a prisoner for life! I am like a caged animal while those who should be imprisoned are free. I feel more and more like an alien. I am suffering a slow torture. I would be better off dead.

CHAPTER 8

Diaspora

We live in an inhospitable world, some would venture to say. For them the world is a danger zone. Apart from disease that can afflict the body there are natural hazards, such as earthquakes, tsunamis and violent storms that can destroy life and property. Apart from natural disasters there may be disasters committed by one's own compatriots or from neighboring lands. Perhaps they do not like the color of your skin or the God to whom you pray or your political opinions. They may be driven to destroy you or to force you out of the land which you might love as much as they do. Survivors have to seek a home elsewhere. There are also others with an insatiable thirst for adventure and curiosity that will search far distant horizons, risking life and limb in their efforts to find a new home for themselves and their families.

On the other hand, imagine a world in which everyone lived in one place peacefully all their lives within an area restricted perhaps by a river, a mountain or the sea, not far from where they were born. Imagine that they lived and played and worked close to the homes of their parents and families, and died approximately in the same neighborhood. One could not travel very far because the territory beyond was unknown, and who knew what dangers lurked there? So it was in days of yore when there was very little movement of people, almost no transportation and fear of survival beyond their known whereabouts. Just beyond their homes there could be enemies, marauders, intruders, wild animals and cannibals, evil spirits and, worst of all, the unknown. No, it was safer to stay at home. If they did stray a little or travel beyond their usual boundaries they would frequently soon return to their nests. But this is not the case in the world in which we live today.

Times have changed. Man has proved himself to be a bold and curious creature. He has traveled and explored and discovered. He has crossed raging rivers and uncharted oceans. He has climbed mountains and descended on the other side into unheard of territory. He has reached the Poles and penetrated tropical jungles. He has even been to the moon and searched for worlds outside this planet. He has built means of transport that have taken him across the land and the seas, the sky and space. Almost no inhabitable part of this earth has been left unnoticed or unclaimed by man. Wherever life could be sustained he has made a home. Maybe, one day, he will find a home outside this planet, too.

Yet there have been and will be those who have left their hearths, not on their own volition. Maybe they were compelled to depart because of tyrannical dictatorships, discrimination or wars or natural catastrophes, famines or conditions that made their continued existence in that place intolerable. They became part of a diaspora - people who left their homelands for different geographical regions, often with a sense of nostalgia and sometimes with the hope and belief that they would return one day to their original homeland when the danger that had caused them to leave was over. The word 'diaspora' comes from the Greek, meaning to sow or to scatter. There have been many mass migrations throughout history, commencing in Biblical days and continuing right to the present – and no doubt, will occur into the future. Man's inhumanity to man has not weakened through the ages. Fortunately there are still other places where one may seek refuge.

In the past diaspora and migration were considered to be different. A diaspora was supposed to consist of people who were forced to leave their homeland unwillingly, but for a long time maintained an urge to return to their own country one day in the future. There was a desire to remember the land of their birth, the language, the songs and dreams and tales of the past, even though these people seldom returned. There was an associated pride intermingled with sadness and nostalgia for their original country of origin which to them had shaped their identity and for which they were proud. A migration, however, did not imply the deep feelings of a diaspora; a migration was merely a change of location usually for practical purposes – a job, a better life or better conditions. The migrant was generally not forced to leave – he left because he decided to go for whatever reason. The invading Barbarians, Tatars and Mongols probably did not want to go back to Siberia or the Gobi Desert. They liked what they saw in the new land. Of late the subtle differences between diaspora and migration have become clouded.

Whether it is diaspora or migration human beings are like migratory birds. However, birds usually return to their original homes whereas humans stay or move even further away. At the end of winter the swallows come back to Capistrano. Humans are different; they are curious, they want to build, they want to gain in wealth and education and they want to make a home for their children – who might not stay because they, too, may want to move on!

There is a flow away from slavery, persecution and dictatorship bringing new thoughts and ideas with the new settlers. Foreign traditions are introduced to the new land, as are foods, arts, crafts and culture. Both diaspora and migration introduce new genes, new ideas and new knowledge, and with that comes advances in understanding and greater development, and a strengthening of the character and moral fiber of the populace. It stimulates physical and mental growth. As the pot boils new flavors and tastes are introduced. A new breath is added to a stagnant atmosphere. Just as consanguineous marriages cause an increase in the development of bad traits so do marriages to foreigners bring on an increase of some of the finer characteristics. Nations, too, thrive on the introduction of foreign blood. Aristotle said that the whole was greater than the sum of its parts.

It is a win-win situation – victory for the immigrant and victory for the adopted land

The history of the Jews is a story of diaspora. Way back in about 2000 BCE, the Bible tells us, Abraham and his family sojourned from Ur in Mesopotamia (present day Iraq), apparently urged to leave by his God who promised that He would lead him to a land flowing with milk and honey, where his offspring would multiply and be like the sands of the desert. He was already unhappy with his father, Terach, who had been trading in idols while Abraham had an inner belief in a single deity. He destroyed his father's idols. He listened to his God's word, and he sojourned to the land of Canaan where he and his followers lived. He married his half-sister Sarah who was infertile for most of her life, but produced her first child Isaac when she was an old woman. Prior to that, she had allowed Abraham to co-habit with her hand-maiden Hagar, who later brought Ishmael into the world. Sarah argued with Hagar and forced Abraham to expel her and her son into the desert, setting off another diaspora whereby we witness the birth of what is known as the Arab nation.

Not until Joseph, the great-grandson of Abraham, was sold into slavery by his brothers who were jealous of him, to a group of travelers going to Egypt, do we hear of a Jewish presence in Egypt. Years later when famine hit the land of Canaan Israelites followed in Joseph's footsteps to Egypt in order to escape the famine, thereby creating a permanent Jewish residence in Egypt. They and their offspring lived in Goshen and were slaves under Pharaoh for five hundred years. They worked in the fields and built forts and structures for grain storage, and did all the hard labor for Pharaoh. One day the Lord commanded Moses to lead the Children of Israel out of Egypt and back to the Holy Land. After traveling through the desert for forty years they finally reached their destination, which was the previous home of their ancestors. They were not driven out of Egypt by the authorities. In fact, they left against the order of the Pharaoh and against their own wishes, too, as they grumbled about leaving a world that they had known, a world where they were fed and felt secure even though they were slaves, for a hazardous trek across an unknown desert inhabited by dangerous war-like tribes so that one day they might arrive at an unknown destination! They complained to Moses that it would have been better to have remained as slaves in Egypt rather than to have been brought to die in the desert. After forty years of traveling and living in the desert and waging many wars with the local inhabitants they finally re-captured their land. Thereafter they lived in the Holy Land for many centuries. First they were ruled by judges, and then by the kings of Israel and Judah.

Once settled in their land they did not travel very far because beyond their borders were hostile tribes that were frequently at war with them. Tarshish, it was said, was the land that was as far west as one could possibly go from the Land of Canaan. Beyond Tarshish there was nothing. It is assumed that Tarshish was Spain, and beyond that the end of the world. Jonah wished to sail there. King Solomon imported luxurious articles, clothing and foods from there. The Phoenicians sailed there from the eastern Mediterranean and traded with the natives, and a number of Jews accompanied them.

After the death of King Solomon many Jews did not wish to accept his son Rehoboam as king, so the Kingdom was split into two countries, Israel and Judea – Judea accepted the new king. The Northern Kingdom of Israel went their own way as a separate state, but was later conquered by the Assyrians who expelled them in about 722 B.C. Some Jews sailed to Tarshish in order to get away from the subjugation of the conquerors. This was the time when the Ten Tribes of Israel disappeared. They probably mingled with the populations in the surrounding lands and some might have returned when matters quieted down. There have been many theories, but no proof, about what happened to the Ten Lost Tribes, ranging from the Mormon teachings that they were the forerunners of the American Indians to other theories that they went to Asia.

Judea was attacked by the Babylonians in the 6th century B.C. This is when the first Temple was destroyed and the Jews were exiled to Babylon; most of them went there but a few decided not to go with the masses and, instead, also sailed to Tarshish where they lived until the Spanish Inquisition.

Those who had been sent to Babylon by Nebuchadnezzar were very unhappy about going there, but they soon settled down, and Babylon became the center of Judaism. It was in Babylon where the intellectual Jews – the rabbis, the teachers and the more wealthy ones - were sent, whereas the poor and the laborers were left in Jerusalem. Babylon became the center of learning; the rabbis and teachers developed schools for studying the Torah and interpreted those statements that the Bible did not fully explain. In fact, it was Babylon where the first synagogues were established and where many religious rites and customs were developed. Babylon became the center of Judaism. The Jews blamed themselves for their expulsion from Jerusalem because they said that they had not followed God's word as well as they should have.

Seventy years after Nebuchadnezzar exiled the Jews to Babylon the Chaldeans (the Babylonians were Chaldeans) themselves were attacked and defeated by the Persians under Cyrus. Cyrus allowed those Jews who wished to return to Jerusalem to do so, but most of them by this time were comfortable enough to remain in Babylon. Those who accepted Cyrus' invitation left Babylon for Jerusalem with Ezra who soon started to re-build the Temple.

The majority who remained behind in Babylon lived under the guidance of a Gaon (an eminent sage and scholar of the Torah). Gaons were always chosen from the descendents of the House of David. In fact, they lived there until well into the 20th century. Only after the State of Israel was established in 1948 and the Arabs turned their hatred towards them did the Iraqi Jews leave Iraq (or Babylon, as it was known) and return to Israel, the land of their ancestors.

However, at one stage, there was a Gaon who died and did not have a son to be his successor. He was therefore followed by his two nephews. One of the nephews was unhappy about sharing his role, so he broke away with his followers, forming the Karaite sect. They believed in the literal Bible without any oral explanations or interpretations by man. A large group of Karaites lived in the Crimean Peninsula, and when the Nazis invaded Crimea in World War II they did not harm the Karaites, because they had decided that Karaites were not Jews.

As Greek civilization exploded and spread throughout the known world the Middle East, too, was swallowed up by them. During the Greek administration of the Holy Land there was a diaspora of Jews to the Greek territories in the Balkans and Asia Minor. They helped to populate these areas, and were influenced by Greek culture even while most of them continued to practice their own religion. The Jews in the Holy Land were impressed with Greek culture and learnt a great deal from them. However, when the Greeks started interfering with the rituals in the Temple the Jews inflicted a humiliating defeat upon them. The Maccabees fought them and took over the administration of the Holy Land, which became known as the Hasmonean Empire. From then onwards Greek influence waned throughout their colonies, so much so that it was not difficult for the Romans to enter and conquer all Greek-owned territories. The Holy Land, too, was finally over-run by the Romans.

The Romans ruled over Palestine (as they called the Holy Land) for many years until the Jews became restive under their occupation. This led to the Jewish War and to the destruction of the Second Temple by the Romans in 67 A.D. Many Jews were taken as slaves to Rome where they served for five years, after which they were set free, thus introducing their DNA into Roman blood.

However, there was another Roman-Jewish War in 137 A.D. Jews had been gradually returning to the Holy Land and re-starting their lives. Hadrian, under the influence of the Greeks, decided to put an end to circumcision which he said was unhealthy. He said he was going to re-build the Temple at the original site, but the Jews soon learned it was to be a Temple to Jupiter. He also changed the name of Jerusalem to Aelia Capitolinia. The Jews under Simon Bar Kokhba, who was considered to be the Messiah, started an uprising against the Romans. After the Romans gathered their troops from between England and the Danube they sent them into Palestine to defeat the Jews at their last bastion, Betar. It is said that a half a million Jews were killed in the war. From that time onwards for many centuries the Jewish center of learning was Babylon as Jerusalem was relatively void of Jews.

By the end of the 4th century A.D. Catholicism became the religion of the Roman Empire thanks to its introduction by Constantine. Under the Catholics Jews were treated poorly; they were prevented from circumcising their young and practicing their rituals. Catholicism was frequently forced upon them and death was the punishment for non-compliance of their demands. Jews were beginning to spread all over Europe, but wherever they went they found that the Catholic Church had preceded them. Life was hard for them in Catholic Europe, but there was nowhere else to turn.

The Middle Ages in Europe were also the Dark Ages and certainly a 'dark' time for Jews. There were attacks and persecution all over Europe, causing Jews to move further eastward. They went to Poland and Lithuania and the Slavic states. Little did they realize that a similar fate awaited them there. The Jews were exiled from France on a few occasions, from Germany and from England by Edward I in 1290. Since Christians were not allowed to become money lenders they at first appreciated the fact that they could borrow from the Jews, but often when it came to re-payment of the debt they complained about their practice of usury. The Jews were blamed for having caused the Black Death. At that time it was not known that the bacteria causing plague were carried by rats, so the Jews were accused of having poisoned the wells in order to spread the disease. Many innocent victims lost their lives on account of this false premise. Jews were accused of the Blood Libel. It was said that they required Christian blood in order to make their matzos for Passover. When a Christian child was missing the Jews were blamed for having taken him for the purpose of matzo production. When the Crusaders went to wrest the Holy Places in Jerusalem from Muslims, the Jews were not left unscathed. They were attacked and killed by the combined forces of Western Europe on their route to Jerusalem. They thought that they would be able to 'kill two birds with one stone', both Muslims and Jews. Jews had to flee for their lives before the oncoming Crusader hordes fell upon them.

The Moors of the Umayyad Dynasty arrived in Babylon in the 7th century, but did not interfere with the religious practices of the Jews. When the Muslims came to Spain in the same century they received a warm welcome from the Jews as they flocked to greet them as they had been mistreated by the Catholics since Christianity had spread there. The Golden Age of Jews in Spain occurred under Muslim rule. They were delighted to be freed from their subjugation under the Christians. The Jews became philosophers, astronomers, doctors and advisers to the Muslim administration. When the Moors went on to invade France (they were turned back by Charles Martel at the gates of Paris) they left the control of the government to the Jews. Despite the relatively good treatment they received from the Muslims there were small pin-pricks such as the dhimmi, which was a tax for non-Muslims and they were not permitted to appear to be higher on their horses than the local Muslims, but these were minor compared to the outrages committed by the previous Catholic rulers. The Jews spoke and wrote their books in Arabic, and some of their works were translated later into Hebrew.

Over the next few hundred years the Catholics gradually retrieved much of their territory from the Muslims, leaving only the southern parts of Spain to them. After the Moors were finally defeated at Cordoba King Ferdinand and Queen Isabella became rulers of the whole of Spain. The Spanish Inquisition exiled all Jews from Spain in 1492, and with that came the next large diaspora. The Jews were horrified by their expulsion because they had been there longer than anyone else, preceding the Catholics by a millennium and Muslims by eight hundred years. The Jews of Toledo asked why they were to be exiled as they had been in Spain (not in Jerusalem) at the time of the Crucifixion, and could not have been responsible for any alleged atrocities against Jesus. The name Toledo even had a Hebrew origin, meaning 'wandering'. Barcelona, Seville and Maqada (from Massada) were all named by the Jews from the Hebrew. They had been so well integrated into Spanish life, and now they were being exiled from their own land by relative foreigners!

This act introduced a massive diaspora to Portugal (thinking that the Inquisition would soon be over, and they would return to their homes), North Africa, Turkey (the Ottoman Empire sent ships to pick up departing Jews from Spain), the Netherlands and, even to the Holy Roman Empire, where they were not very popular. Most important of all, they trailed Columbus, and populated the Caribbean Islands and South America, assisting in the early development of these lands. The Inquisition, however, followed them from Spain to Portugal, and later to the Portuguese colony of Brazil and the Spanish possessions in the Caribbean.

Anti-Semitism in Europe created bitter living conditions, especially in countries like Poland where Jews constituted large percentages of the population in many of the towns. There were pogroms in Eastern Europe and forced military service in the Russian army. Toward the end of the nineteenth century they started moving away from the danger zones, mostly to America.

The next large exodus of Jews followed World War II. The Nazis tried very hard to eliminate the Jewish population of Europe, and were almost successful. They exterminated six million European Jews. Those Jews who had been fortunate enough to escape the death camps, the ovens and gas chambers required a home, and as luck would have it in 1948 the United Nations divided Palestine into a Jewish and an Arab homeland. Jews had been trickling into Palestine prior to and during the war despite British attempts to prevent their entry. Now that they had a land that they could call their own, which was sanctioned by a world body of nations, they were suddenly confronted by an Arab invasion from all sides. At least half a dozen Arab nations participated in this attack. With an untrained incomplete army and an unprepared leadership they were able to stave off the Arab onslaught.

This was only the beginning of a series of invasions that failed, and constant rocket attacks which Israel has had to endure. The wars between Arabs and Jews created almost a million refugees on both sides, since many Jews lived in Arab lands and an equal number of Arabs resided in Israel. The only difference is that Israel absorbed every Jewish refugee from neighboring Arab countries immediately whereas after more than sixty-five years the Arab refugees from 1948, together with their children and grand-children in the interim, still remain refugees living in camps because the host Arab lands will not absorb them – or they do not wish to be absorbed. In a short half century since its inception the land of Israel has forged ahead into an advanced modern industrialized, scientific and technological nation. The Palestinians could have made similar advances as half the land was given to them, but instead the Arabs preferred to complain, go to war and remain permanent refugees while resenting the Jewish presence.

There was an infusion of Soviet Jewry into Israel in the late 20th century. The Soviets were a religion-free country. Jews – and other peoples - were not allowed to practice their religion openly. Jews were not being circumcised, there were no synagogues there and they were losing touch with their rituals of the past. Many had wanted to emigrate but were not permitted to do so until large protests and marches and pressure from the free world influenced the Soviet authorities to relax their grip and let the people go. They migrated mainly to the US and Israel. A smaller but considerably large-sized group of Jews were airlifted from Addis Ababa, Ethiopia to Israel under similar circumstances.

So we see that diaspora can be best explained by relating the history of the 'wandering' Jews. The Jew has spent the major part of the history of civilization being persecuted and searching for a new home.

Of course, diaspora is not a re-location of peoples applying only to Jews. It probably has occurred in almost all countries of the world at some time or other and will continue to do so into the future. The results of such movements of people are usually for the good as an influx of new blood frequently injects fresh ideas, adds willing hands and a positive outlook for the nation. Without immigration people might become stale, bored and idle, and advances into the modern era might fall behind. Re-location of populations is as healthy and cleansing as the tides of the ocean or the steady flow of a river to the sea or a gentle breeze over land. It brings in the new while diluting the old. It introduces innovation and progress. It is like the changing of the seasons or the introduction of fresh air into a stuffy room. Nations that have new immigrants and new genes frequently fare better than those whose populations remain stagnant.

Since the sixteenth century when new continents were opened up Europe has spilled millions of its inhabitants throughout the world, also populating the Americas. Africans have been sold into slavery, especially to the Americas and to the islands of the Caribbean. Indians and Chinese have left Asia to find work and to create a better life for themselves and their children, permeating through every land on all the continents and their islands. Today the Americas can boast of being the home to peoples from every corner of the earth.

During the Iron Age the British Isles were inhabited by Britons. Where did they come from? Probably from the European mainland – some say originally from Armenia. They resisted the Roman invasion in about 43 A.D., but soon became willing subjects of the Roman Empire. The Romans stayed there until the beginning of the 5th century A.D., whereupon there was an onslaught of Angles and Saxons who came from Germany. These new invaders settled in the British Isles and controlled the southern part of England until the Norman conquest by William the Conqueror (who was invited) in 1066. In the meantime there had been many attacks by the Vikings, and even after William the Conqueror had organized the country under his rule the Danes raided again, but went home after William paid them a large sum of money. Usually when the invaders arrived most of them did not return home, but remained, mixed with the people and introduced alien blood into the population. So we see that the British Isles, apart from its original inhabitants, received injections of German, French and Scandinavian blood. The English language, too, received injections of words and expressions from these new members of their population, who have contributed to the richness and wide range of the English language.

In the nineteenth century Ireland was a part of the British Empire. The Irish were not treated well by the English. They were Catholic and poor while the rest of the British Isles were Protestant. Henry VIII of England had long ago broken away from the Catholic Church; this had brought on a rivalry between the Church of England and the Catholics. The Irish were not allowed to own land in their own country. The land was owned by the English landlords, who were usually absentee landlords. The Irish were prevented from voting or receiving an education or becoming professionals. They were looked down upon as an inferior race. The Irish worked the land and sustained themselves with the crops they grew. These crops were generally potatoes. In 1845 after a good spring and summer they expected a fine potato crop, but what they brought up from the land was pure inedible mush. Blight, caused by a fungus, had hit the potato harvest. The same happened the next few years. Potatoes were a major part of the Irish diet. Britain did not care much about the suffering of the Irish farmers and their families, and did very little to help them out of their misery. They also thought that the Irish should find a resolution to their own problems. Britain treated its Empire more as a large business than as a Commonwealth of mutual aid. Even today it is still being debated as to whether genocide was committed by the British upon the Irish by doing nothing to assist them in their plight. Surely, the Irish said, if the potato blight had occurred in an English county the British government would have assisted them.

It is surprising that the potato blight caused such havoc upon Ireland as other crops were also grown there, but these were exported to Britain and other parts of the world because there was more money available from export than from selling those crops within Ireland. Cornmeal was sent to them from North America but they did not have the mills to convert it to flour, so they could not use it. One million people died from the potato famine and one million people migrated to other parts of the British Isles and the North American continent. Ireland's population was decreased by 25%. This is when the Gaelic language also suffered a severe blow because the lands to which the Irish emigrated had no need for a language of the Middle Ages. They had come mostly from western Ireland where Gaelic was the predominant tongue. From that time onwards the Irish independence movements started growing, and that led to the development of an independent Irish Republic in the 20th century.

The diaspora from Ireland added a new ingredient into the melting pot that helped shape North America as the home of fugitives from poverty and religious intolerance of the Old World. The north-eastern portion of the United States became the home of most of the Irish immigrants.

What better example of diaspora is there than the growth of the United States? More than fifteen thousand years ago the American continent was devoid of people. It was like the moon or Mars. Unlike Africa there is no sign of the origins of mankind on the American continent. Fifteen thousand years ago the first migration from Siberia occurred. This took place over the Bering Straits which was a land mass during the Ice Age. The people swept southwards hugging the Pacific coast, some branching off every now and then and populating different parts of the continent. In a process lasting hundreds of years the people went southwards as far as South America, even arriving at the southern tip. They enjoyed a pastoral and nomadic life. There were other migrations through the Bering Straits, less widespread and less spectacular, one of which remained mostly in the north of North America, constituting mainly the Eskimos, Aleuts and Inuits. Apparently there were some reverse migrations, too, where some went back to Siberia.

It appears as though five hundred years before Columbus, Leif Erickson, a Norse-man, sailing from Greenland landed on the north-eastern shores of Canada, probably Labrador and Baffin Land. However, the Norse did not create lasting settlements on the continent. Not until Christopher Columbus arrived did civilization as we know it settle its roots into the Americas. Suddenly a flood of immigrants invaded the Caribbean islands and the mainland of South America. The first European immigrants came from Spain and Portugal, arriving in the islands of the Caribbean and then on the South American mainland. This included Jews escaping from the Spanish and Portuguese Inquisitions who came to the Caribbean islands and Brazil, not anticipating that the Inquisition would follow them there, too.

Religious persecution has been a primary reason for the departure of many hundreds of thousands of people from their native lands and caused them to seek a new home on unexplored shores. It seems very strange that people worshipping the same God should be persecuted by their fellow countrymen because they might do so in a different way. The Pilgrims sailed from England because the Church of England would not allow them to practice their religion in a simpler way, without the embellishments of beautiful churches and their stain-glassed windows. They wished to serve their God in the manner in which it was written in the Bible. In 1620 they arrived in Cape Cod; they actually intended to sail to Virginia where a colony had already been established, but decided to stay where they landed as their food had run out and their ship, the Mayflower, was in poor condition. Decades later they were followed by the Puritans who came for similar reasons, saying that the Church of England was only partially removed from Catholicism, and they wanted a clean break.

During the Reformation the Huguenots of France followed the teachings of John Calvin rather than the Catholic Church, but they were attacked and killed, and a war was fought against them by the Catholics. Finally at the Edict of Nantes in 1598 peace was announced and the Huguenots were allowed some autonomy. In 1620 Louis XIV revoked the Treaty. Three-quarters of the Huguenots were killed and a half a million escaped from the land of their birth and traveled to many different countries in Europe, North and as far afield as South Africa. Wherever they went they brought their artistry and craft-work and winery techniques which improved the outputs of their adopted lands and diminished those of France by their departure.

Before the Mayflower came to Cape Cod the British arrived in Virginia where they had a hard time surviving because of climatic conditions and their inexpert abilities in farming, as well as their difficulties in handling bellicose native Americans. At one stage the colony was abandoned.

Over time the Spanish, the Dutch and the French arrived in North America. There was no need for them to go back as they found more potential here than they had even dreamed of. They came for land and for adventure, for gold and for hunting, for religious tolerance and a new life. The Native Americans began to feel hemmed in, attacked, and feared the loss of their land. Wars followed as each side tried to hold on to their territories. Gradually the natives retreated, leaving the land to the newcomers.

Almost every European and Asian country has contributed to the polyglot population of the Americas. People have escaped from persecution by the czars, tyrants, governments, pogroms and poverty, and have come to seek a better life of freedom and wealth. Yet even persecutors hiding under new identities while escaping recognition and trials, such as Nazi war criminals after World War II found refuge in the Americas and elsewhere. The American continent has been a land of refuge not only for the persecuted, but also for the persecutor. Adolph Eichman and many of his Nazi cronies found refuge in South America where they hid and were protected by their hosts.

Wars, droughts and famines have caused millions of Chinese to leave their homelands and move into the lands all around the Pacific Rim and even bordering the Indian Ocean. Hard work and diligence accompanied their migrations. If not for Chinese labor the Trans-Continental Railroad in the USA might have not been built so soon and so cheaply. This was the beginning of a Chinese presence in America.

In many instances in the past huge hordes of people have moved across continents, like African antelope stampeding in search of water. When Alexander the Great became the foremost leader of his time by conquering most of the known world Hellenism spread throughout North Africa, southern Europe and Asia like wildfire. His people did not have a hankering to return to their homeland but made lives for themselves in the conquered territories. They occupied the Balkans and Asia Minor, introducing their culture, language, philosophy, gymnastics and their worship of the human body to an area that sorely lacked such education.

Other huge movements of large populations occurred in Europe. The Magyars came from Siberia and invaded Hungary round about the 5th century, giving Hungarians a language unrelated to any other European language, except for Finnish. Scandinavians traveled eastward and westward; the Vikings went west as far as Greenland and to the American continent while their brothers went east into Russia, and were known as the Rus. They spread throughout Russia, introducing their blonde skins and culture to the Slavs and Tatars in Asia and Western Europe. Goths, Vandals, Angles and Saxons invaded Germany and Central Europe. A second wave of Barbarians consisting of Slavs and Bulgars followed them, conquering those who came before and adding their genes to the people already there.

In those days nation states were not as demarcated as they are today. People were more tribal; they followed their leaders, and their common language held them together. Mountains and rivers and artificial borders did not hold them back; they followed their tribes. Hence when the Middle East was divided amongst the European nations in the middle of the nineteenth century many Arabs from a particular clan found themselves living with another clan with whom they had nothing in common, only because the new colonial powers had clumped them together within new borders.

There was a major migration from Africa that lasted about three hundred years. To call it a diaspora would be misusing the word. This was not an escape from persecution but a sale for profit where millions of black people were sold as slaves, like cattle, to the North and South American markets and the Caribbean islands. The export of Africans as slaves was started in the fifteenth century by the Portuguese who had been hugging the coast of Africa in their attempts at exploring the continent. They captured and brought slaves to the coast of Guinea and the island of Sao Tome to do the arduous work on the sugar plantations – work that was shunned by the Portuguese people. Then the Spaniards brought slaves to Cuba and Hispaniola, where many died during the Atlantic crossing in large numbers from salt depletion and starvation under the hot equatorial sun. Water, water everywhere, but not a drop to drink! More slaves were required to replace those lost and for the expansion of plantations and businesses.

The slave trade became a huge operation as they had to be bought from African chieftains and Arab traders. The Triangular Slave Trade came into being. Goods came from Europe to supply the chieftains in exchange for black people who were captured like animals from as far as hundreds of miles away; these were then shipped to Europe and the Americas. It was a lucrative trade for the chieftains and for the White slave traders and lasted well into the 19th century. It will be remembered as a dark period in the history of human morality and ethics. The guilt must be shared between the White slave traders, Arab intermediaries and the African chieftains who sold their people for profit and the slave owners who exacted every bit of work that they could get out of them and gave so little to them in return. This practice reached its peak in the 18th century. African empires led by chieftains were formed as a result of the slave trade, but when abolition of slavery finally took place these empires crumbled.

In the seventeenth century Southern Africa was a barren wasteland. There was a sparse population of unclothed Stone Age people, the Koi, Bushmen and Hottentots, hunter-gatherers living mainly on roots and berries and the rare animal poisoned by a curare-like substance through a stab-wound or primitive arrow. The Bantu of South Africa had not yet arrived as they were still further to the north, an area where the White man would later explore. Bartholomew Diaz and Vasco Da Gama had rounded the Cape at the southern tip of Africa, but this did not initiate a surge of immigration. Only after the Dutch East India Company used the route around Africa to do business with their valuable Asian trading partners did they realize that their sailors were coming down with scurvy because of a lack of fresh fruit and vegetables. The Dutch under Jan van Riebeek set up a colony at the tip of the African continent in 1652 mostly for the purpose of developing fruit and vegetable gardens to feed their sailors in order to prevent scurvy. This Halfway House was to be a replenishing source of these essential commodities. Soon Dutch farmers arrived there to set up farms for their own purposes. They were joined by the French Huguenots who were Protestants that had suffered from religious persecution at the hands of the Catholics at home. A steady stream of settlers from the Netherlands, France and Germany migrated to the Cape Province.

As there was a limited source of labor available at the Cape – the Koi would not react to organized directives from anybody - Malay workers were brought in from the territories of the Dutch East India Company. These Malays made the southern tip of Africa their home and constitute a large percentage of the present colored population of South Africa.

During the Napoleonic Wars the Dutch, fearing that they may lose the land to the French, gave the territory known as the Cape Colony to the British for temporary safe-keeping in view of their phenomenal sea power. The territory never reverted back to Dutch control. The Dutch settlers who by now were known as Afrikaners became discontented with the British authorities. The British were indifferent to the conflicts that the border Afrikaner farmers living in the Eastern Cape Province were undergoing as a result of raids by the Xhosa people on their farms for cattle and agricultural products. Abolition of slavery in 1834 and the poor compensation given to slave owners was another problem, even though most Afrikaners did not even own slaves. A sticking point was that slaves were given equal rights as Christians which was contrary to

God's will, so they said. To add insult to injury the Koi were allowed to marry in Church, which was anathema to the Boers (Afrikaner farmers). They also complained that they had no or very little representation in the government; they had no security and they were made to feel inferior. They soon became Anglophobic. Therefore, they decided to trek into the interior.

Historically this was known as the Great Trek – an arduous journey. They wanted their freedom and wished to practice their own religion (Dutch Reformed Church); they also wished to govern themselves. They encountered numerous hazards crossing mountains and swollen rivers in their ox-wagons. They defended themselves in what was known as lagers, where they placed all the wagons in a circle while they were protected within, and fired at the oncoming marauders between the wagons and the wheel-spokes. There were many marauders in the way of African tribes with whom they came into contact for the first time.

They started three separate republics in Natal, Transvaal and the Orange Free State. In order to set up an area for themselves in Natal they made arrangements with Dingaan, the Zulu chief, who initially stated that he was prepared to cede to them some land that they had requested. They were invited into the living quarters of Dingaan in order to sign the papers. Once they entered the quarters Dingaan's men fell upon them and slaughtered each one of them. In 1838 at the Battle of Blood River the Afrikaners avenged this foul deed and set up the Republic of Natal. Unfortunately, in 1843 Britain took over Natal. The Transvaal and the Orange Free State republics lasted somewhat longer.

The Great Trek opened up the southern part of the African continent for exploration, industrialization and emigration. An empty land was transformed into an agricultural, industrial and mining country, acting as a magnet for new settlers. In the middle of the 19th century diamonds were discovered in Kimberley, and in 1886 gold was found in Johannesburg. Gold- and diamond-mining attracted hordes of people from all corners of the world to come and seek their fortunes. South Africa became the largest producer of gold and diamonds in the world. Related industries developed and grew side by side with the heavy metals making South Africa into the most industrialized country on the African continent.

Britain went to war against the Boer Republics, supposedly to protect the rights of the immigrant miners, but probably for the gold and diamonds and real estate. This was the age of Empire-building. In 1902, after three years of fighting, Britain took over the Boer Republics, and brought South Africa into the British Empire.

South Africa became a haven for British and Dutch citizens who wanted to improve their lives and were willing to begin a new life. Many Jews from Eastern Europe, having suffered from the pogroms in Russia and Poland, and in order to escape mandatory service in the Russian army (for which they felt no loyalty) found in South Africa a home where the climate was mild, good jobs available and living conditions better than what they had known in the past; and there was no persecution. Many Indians, who had been leaving their homeland for centuries and spreading along the Pacific Rim and its islands and the shores of the Indian Ocean, were now arriving on the east coast of Natal. At first, they came to work on the sugar cane plantations, and then they brought their families. South Africa became a land of opportunity and hope.

When India gained its independence from Britain it was initially intended that it should be one country, but Muslims fought for separation from Hindus. With the partition into India and Pakistan and after the killing of tens of thousands of people in 1948 numerous Muslims left India for Pakistan and a similar number of Hindus went from Pakistan to India. This involved the re-location of millions of people. India, a Hindu country, still remains the second most populous Muslim country in the world; only Indonesia can boast a larger Muslim population. Since partition India and Pakistan have fought a number of wars caused by religious strife and for control of the Punjab, home of both Hindus and Muslims.

The Vietnam War saw millions of Vietnamese seeking new homes in America and other countries. After years of blood-shed and genocide many of these war-weary people sought a new life away from the killing fields. The same could be said for Cambodians and Laotians who suffered similar fates in their own countries. The Iranian Revolution, too, following the deposition of the Shah sent many Iranians out of the country. Those who did not cherish living in a theocracy migrated to other lands to start life anew.

In the early part of the 21st century as a result of the Iraq and Afghan Wars numerous people were displaced by the exigencies of war, and were forced to flee to other parts of Asia and the US in order to start a new life. Syria has already lost 4 million people who left their homes as refugees from the war which has involved a few different factions – Assad slaughtering Sunnis while Islamists are trying to set up a caliphate in Northern Syria and Iraq. Jordan and Turkey are strewn with refugee camps holding those who have escaped from the war and those who will not fight for Assad. These displaced persons are a drain on the host populations who have to feed and shelter them. They are not admitted as citizens while their futures are in limbo. Jordan and Lebanon, too, have tens of thousands of Palestinian refugees living in tents for the past half century. The host countries will not admit them as citizens. The population of Jordanian citizens in Jordan is by far a minority as compared to the number of Syrian, Iraqi and Palestinian refugees that it harbors.

Sri Lanka, too, had a Civil War, with Tamils and Singhalese killing each other. A similar dispersion of populations occurred there. When China invaded Tibet it was not only the Dalai Lama who fled; he was followed by numerous Tibetans who escaped to India and other countries.

The reign of Idi Amin sent many Ugandans out of the country to neighboring lands in order to seek a better life away from a blood-thirsty dictator. This also occurred when the Hutu and Tootsies of Rwanda performed genocide upon each other causing numerous survivors to seek asylum elsewhere. There, too, was a diaspora from Cuba after the Castro overthrow of the Batista government. Huge numbers of Cubans who did not want to live under a Communist regime migrated to the United States, most of them settling in Miami. Transfer of populations followed the numerous civil wars and forceful coups that occurred in many South America countries throughout the 19th and 20th centuries.

Australia, a continental land-mass on the other side of the world, is populated by migrants who arrived there in the last three hundred years. The original aboriginal people had been living 'down under' for about fifty thousand years, but nobody knows for certain how they arrived there as the sixty miles of sea (the Torres Straits) between Papua and the north of Australia is very rough and the seamen of those days probably did not have the ability to cross it. However, there have been times when the seas were at lower levels, and by utilizing the islands in between it could have been possible in the presence of low tides to make the crossing.

The British laid claim to Australia in 1770, and in 1788 commenced to send ship-loads of prisoners to the land. These are prisoners who would have been sent to its colonies in North America, but since they broke away after the War of Independence the British delivered the convicts to Australia. The prisoners from the penal colony were the first White Australians. These were followed by non-prisoner citizens from the British Isles. World War II introduced a large number of New Australians onto the continent, both from the British Isles and Europe. From a rocky start as a penal colony Australia has developed into a modern industrialized country and an example to the world as a free and peaceful democracy. Asians for a long time were barred from becoming Australian citizens; but this has changed, and today there is an increasing Asian population in the country. Virtually, all non-aboriginal Australians are migrants – as are all non-native Americans!

History is full of the story of migrating populations, almost like migratory birds – but the birds usually return home with the change in the seasons; this is not the case with people of the diaspora. We see that there is a constant movement of people to seek safety for their families and freedom to live with a desire to earn a livelihood. Like the birds and the animal kingdom man, too, has his predators. Birds and animals are usually hunted for food by larger and stronger species or by man for food or plumes or pelts or horns, but man is frequently killed by his fellow man because of his religious beliefs (even if he worships the same God, but in a different way), political convictions or the color of his skin.

Migration and diaspora of people today is somewhat different to what it was in days gone by. Countries have borders but people do not. When, in the past, they left one country and went to the next they often lost touch with their friends and their families but today they can land in the new country and immediately get on to their cell phones and call their loved ones as often as they wish to as if they had been living down the road. They can see them on Skype as though they are in the same room. They can receive or send money to each other, and even do business with each other, introducing new ideas from the adopted land. Cheap flights will bring them back to their friends and families as often as they please. The world is shrinking, and we are becoming more of a global community.

You need only to walk down a street in a large city in order to see a multitude of different faces from all over the world and hear the variety of languages spoken. Never before has there been such an admixture of race and color and religion. The world is becoming more 'global'. There are more Irish living outside Ireland than in Ireland. Chinese have spread throughout South-East Asia and Indians down the eastern coast of Africa. The British Empire has brought Britons to all countries of the world as has colonial France brought the French to North Africa. Muslims have 'invaded' Europe, and given it an Islamic face that has never been seen before, even in the Golden days of Islam. In fact, this planet is becoming more cosmopolitan, despite laws and boundaries set up by man. Cities in different countries are beginning to resemble each other.

At the present time we are witnessing shiploads of people leaving the lands of their birth at great personal risk, in rickety vessels and flimsy rafts in order to escape wars, autocratic regimes and murderous terrorist groups. They are sailing across the Mediterranean from the Middle East and Africa. Thousands of lives have been lost at sea due to the unseaworthy craft being employed, and those who are fortunate enough to arrive in a foreign country are generally not welcome as they consist of ship-loads of more mouths to feed, people with jobs to be found in a market which already has a high unemployment rate, and an economy with fewer jobs because of computerization and modern technology.

Perhaps, amongst these migrants there may be some terrorists who one day might be on their way to join terrorist brigades, thus constituting a security risk. The same is happening in Myanmar where the Rohingya Muslims (who originally came from Bengal and migrated to Burma) are being persecuted by the Buddhists. Large numbers have been sailing to Thailand to escape their hard lives, but there have been numerous drownings at sea and little hope for those who have arrived on dry land.

Imagine the terror of these escapees from wars and hunger and fear searching for a haven in the unknown, traveling in rickety vessels, which they know are unsafe, for a destination – should they ever arrive there alive- where they are aware that they are illegal migrants and unwanted! Imagine the desperation of these people!

Can we say that immigration is always a force for the good? No, we cannot say that. There are times when criminals, thieves, murderers and other shady characters may leave their own lands and enter another country legally or illegally, and continue to wreak havoc with a life of crime and sin. There are those who, because of laziness or lack of education or inexperience may also turn to a life of crime and sin and anti-social and anti-government behavior where they fill up the jails and are under constant police vigilance. They may sometimes introduce the use and sale of illegal drugs, increase sex trafficking and can become a national safety hazard.

At this time in 2015 we read in the newspapers and hear on radio and television of the fraternal wars in the Middle East and North Africa. Iraq has been through a ten year war and Afghanistan's war has been longer. Syria is in the midst of a struggle between Sunni and Shiites. Iran is surreptitiously aiding the Shia. Turkey is bombing her own people, the Kurds. Boca Haram in North Africa is in control of large areas of Nigeria and Mali. Yemen is smoldering. Al Qaeda continues to threaten and attack their brethren who do not agree with them. Fundamentalist religious orders and nationalistic groups are creating dangerous living conditions all over the Middle East and North Africa. The Islamic State grabs more Syrian and Iraqi territory. No wonder that there have been so many deaths and millions of displaced persons - refugees from these lands trying to enter other countries, mostly in Europe, the closest to them.

This is a huge problem. We notice that the Arab countries in the Middle East have not welcomed them. Saudi Arabia and the Arab Emirates have not lifted a finger. Should the nations of Europe and America absorb these poor souls? They are in a desperate plight. Yet we know that they hate Americans and Jews and Israel and Christianity. We also know that many cities in Europe, such as Rotterdam and Marseilles have more Muslim children under the age of sixteen than non-Muslim. At noon-time many of the streets of Paris are closed to traffic because it is time for Muslim prayers which are being carried out on the street. They have brought with them to Europe a virulent form of anti-Semitism that has influenced the spread of Jew-hatred. We also know that Islamic terrorists have attacked cities like New York, London, Paris and Madrid for political reasons and caused much physical damage and fear in the hearts of the citizens. We have heard of numerous Muslims from Europe who have gone to fight for the Islamic state with whom we are at war. How many of these new Muslim refugees who might be admitted to European countries and the USA will be enrolling to fight for the Islamic State? Once they enter European countries in large numbers they will ask for – as they have done in London and Paris and Amsterdam – Shariah Law (religious law) which often conflicts with the law of the land of their adoption. Yes, it is only right to adopt a refugee who is fleeing for his life, but at what a price!

So we see that the story of diaspora is the history of mankind. In the majority of cases it is for the good, but at certain times it could be disastrous!

Printed in the United States
By Bookmasters